Restless Spirits

Restless Spirits

plays

William S. Yellow Robe Jr.

edited by
Jace Weaver

Foreword by
Hanay L. Geiogamah

excelsior editions

AN IMPRINT OF STATE UNIVERSITY OF NEW YORK PRESS

Cover art: *Christina's World* by Brent Learned. Printed with permission.

Published by State University of New York Press, Albany

© 2020 William S. Yellow Robe Jr.

All rights reserved

No part of this book may be used or reproduced in any manner whatsoever without written permission. No part of this book may be stored in a retrieval system or transmitted in any form or by any means including electronic, electrostatic, magnetic tape, mechanical, photocopying, recording, or otherwise without the prior permission in writing of the publisher.

Excelsior Editions is an imprint of State University of New York Press

For information, contact State University of New York Press, Albany, NY
www.sunypress.edu

Library of Congress Cataloging-in-Publication Data

Names: Yellow Robe, William S., [date] – author. | Weaver, Jace, [date] – editor.
Title: Restless spirits : plays / William S. Yellow Robe Jr., edited by
  Jace Weaver.
Description: Albany : State University of New York Press, [2020] | Series:
  Excelsior editions
Identifiers: LCCN 2019028972 | ISBN 9781438478647 (pbk. : alk. paper) | ISBN
  9781438478630 (ebook)
Classification: LCC PS3575.E46 A6 2020 | DDC 812/.54—dc23
LC record available at https://lccn.loc.gov/2019028972

10 9 8 7 6 5 4 3 2 1

Contents

Foreword / vii
by Hanay L. Geiogamah

Production Histories / ix

Introduction / 1

Wood Bones / 7

Frog's Dance / 99

Falling Distance / 147

Wink-Dah / 173

To Cross / 227

It Came from Across the Big Pond / 237

The Curse of the Tiger Lily Two-Step / 259

One Step In / 277

Notes / 285

Foreword

HANAY L. GEIOGAMAH

For so long, I have viewed the work of William S. Yellow Robe Jr. as very dark, very nearly too bleak, disturbing, and uncomfortable. As I finished reading the manuscript for the collection you now hold in your hands, I think I have had a new insight and understanding of his vision and aim as a playwright.

Bill has undertaken to explore the internal dynamics of the dislocated spiritual and physical grimness that has attached itself for centuries like a super-powerful leech to American Indian existence. In the words of a Johnny Cash song, he writes about "the mud and the blood and the beer."

This exploration, courageous and unwavering, has covered human tragedy and failure ranging from incest, racism, murder, vengeful ghosts and spirits, child molestation, rape, homosexual ritual suicide, madness, alcohol-induced necrophilia, and all sorts of vermin and varmints. It is all there in his body of work, and it is all legitimate and real. These things are happening to his characters in straightforward contexts and are not meant to provoke sci-fi or horror scares for shock value alone.

What is especially of note about Bill's theatrical journeys into this dark terrain is his careful and methodical search for glimmers and sudden flashes of truth, honesty, decency, tradition, and respect that are somehow embedded there as sharp fragments of a larger, atavistic code of life that has largely vanished for most American Indians. When he grabs hold of a chunk of this stuff, the poet in Bill weaves it—with his personal brand of Indian humor and wit—into the narrative. Bill is expert in the application of some of Indian humor's more mordant expressions. Every Yellow Robe play contains a sharp kick, a gut punch, a jab, an unexpected lurch, and these plays all exhibit various representations of these elements.

❧

The editor, Professor Jace Weaver, has organized the flow of these plays in a progression that provides both a subtle thematic undertow and also a contrasting mixture of the ghostly, spiritual, and fantastical characters and situations. He is to be commended for working with Bill to assemble this group of plays—this is a real gift to the American Indian theater—and to theater, more generally.

A discernible wisp of playfulness emanates from the restless spirits we encounter in this collection, prompting one to consider if Bill just might be feeling a little bit more hopeful about some things. His play *Wink-Dah* is a powerful, shocking experience that contains much of this approach, a shuddering play that somehow manages to articulate a gentle, courageous whisper of hope in the face of a certain and grisly death.

Bill is the American Indian theater's lead scout into the darker, more haunted corners of Native life, in the past and in the present. His works are reminiscent of Poe and Arrabal, Genet, and even a bit of Yeats. Bill's courage as a writer has always provided stark originality in his work, and one can easily say that there are no other plays in the American theater like his plays. This collection confirms Mr. Yellow Robe's ranking at the top of the line among American Indian dramatists. He is gifted with a special kind of creative sophistication. His plays, challenging as they really and truly are, should be read by many, many American Indians, especially those who want to understand the complete, and I believe, redeeming truth.

Production Histories

The production histories for this collection of plays are varied. Some of the plays have been in production and readings for several years, while others are very new. I have always found production histories informing but cold. In breaking that mode, I would like to take this time to thank the people who have supported these plays and the work. My way of saying, "*pinamiya*": Bob Jaffe, Madeline Sayet, Dawn Jamison, Victor Ryan Pierce, Veracity Butcher, Freedome Bradley-Ballentine, Albert Ybarra, Maulian Dana, Margo Lukens, Amy Roeder, George Theriault, Sophia Dalleo, Dale Lolar, Sierra Crosby, Michelle Benard, Keith Conway, Joseph Grady, Ruth Swaney, Bill Swaney, David L. Moore, Jarvis Sandoval, Lisa Roth, Morgan Jenness, Daniel Banks, Shelia Rocha, Jace Weaver, and Jeanne Domek. Theaters and organizations: Thunderbird Theatre, New Native Theatre, Lark Development, the Eagle Project, AS220, and 4 to 1 Path Productions.

Wood Bones

Produced by School of Performing Arts, University of Maine, Orono, ME, November 2017.

Directed by William S. Yellow Robe Jr, featuring Currant Grant, Sierra Crosby, Carmella Bear, Isabella Etro, Emma Nichols, Brady Lambert, and Zachary Peacock; produced by Haskell Indian Nations University, Thunderbird Theatre, Lawrence, KS, April 2016.

Produced by the Eagle Project, directed by Bob Jaffe, June Havoc Theatre at the Abingdon Theatre Arts Complex, New York, NY, May 2013.

Development Reading, directed by Bob Jaffe, Lark Play Development, Lark Play Development Studios, New York, NY, June 2012.

Reading, produced by the Eagle Project, directed by Bob Jaffe, North Studio, the Playwrights Horizons, New York, NY, March 2012.

Reading, produced by American Indian Repertory Theatre, directed by Diane Yeahquo Reyner, Lawrence Arts Center Black Box Theater, Lawrence, KS, February 2011.

Frog's Dance

Reading, produced by Tan Kttotsanin, New Native Tribal Plays, directed by Madeline Sayet, Penobscot Theater Rehearsal Space, Bangor, ME, April 2017.

Reading, directed by Marcia Douglas, University of Maine, Orono, ME, May 2017.

Reading, produced by the Bearhead Swaney Inter-Tribal Playwrights' Center, directed by William S. Yellow Robe Jr., Arlee, MT, August 2014.

Falling Distance

Reading, University of Maine, directed by William S. Yellow Robe Jr., Orono, ME, October 2007.

Reading, produced by No Borders Indigenous Inter-Tribal Theater Company, directed by William S. Yellow Robe Jr., AS220, Providence, RI, August 2003.

Wink-Dah

Directed by Rich Litchie, Ensemble Studio Theater, "Marathon of One Acts," directed by Rich Litchie, New York, NY, May 1989.

Directed by Christina Yao, American Conservatory Theater, "Plays in Progress" series, San Francisco, CA, November 1988.

To Cross

First draft.

It Came from Across the Big Pond

First draft.

The Curse of the Tiger Lily Two-Step

First draft.

One Step In

Directed by Rhiana Yazzie, featuring: Alan Gross, Elizabeth Gates, and Rhian Yazzie, the New Native Theatre's National Native American Ten-Minute Play Festival, Minneapolis, MN, August 2017.

Reading. Directed by William S. Yellow Robe Jr., Returning the Gift Literary Festival, University of Oklahoma, Norman, OK, October 2017.

Introduction

I hate to begin this introduction to a collection of plays by William S. Yellow Robe Jr. by breaking some bad news. Bill Yellow Robe is not a great Native American playwright. He is not even a great Assiniboine playwright. This will no doubt strike most readers as odd. Do not misunderstand me. He is unquestionably Native American, Assiniboine, and a playwright. But he is not a great Native American playwright. Bill Yellow Robe is quite simply a great American playwright.

In the nineteenth century, a common lament was, "Where is the African Shakespeare?" Albert Schweitzer famously called Nobel Laureate Rabindranath Tagore the Indian Goethe. And Saul Bellow, in defending himself against charges of racial insensitivity, wrote in the *New York Times*, "There is no Bulgarian Proust. Have I offended Bulgarians too?"[1] In each case there is the clear implication that the writer in need of the adjectival modifier is inferior to the *real* Shakespeare, the *real* Proust, or the *real* Goethe. To label someone a great Native American playwright, as accurate as that identification may be, is to pigeonhole and limit him or her, again making that person less than a great American playwright—or better yet, simply a great playwright. Bill Yellow Robe is a great American playwright, in the company of other great contemporary American playwrights like David Mamet, Lynn Nottage, David Rabe, Wallace Shawn, and Pearl Cleage.

Yellow Robe has written over sixty plays in a career that spans nearly forty years. There have been two previous anthologies of his plays, *Where the Pavement Ends* (2000) and *Grandchildren of the Buffalo Soldiers* (2009). There has been none in the ensuing decade, which represents one his most creative and productive periods. Hence the need for the collection you hold in your hands.

He is the best Native playwright working today, in the vein of Hanay Geiogamah and Tomson Highway. Birgit Dawes, in her entry on him in *The*

Methuen Drama Guide to Contemporary American Playwrights, states, "Even though realism—in the tradition of Eugene O'Neill and Sam Shepard—is his signature format," his plays often "also explore mythical, magic realist, and satirical strategies." The entry also noted that he was one of the most visible and frequently produced Native artists.[2] Geiogamah, arguably the founder of contemporary Native drama, praises Yellow Robe for his " 'courageous determination to dramatize some of the harsher truths of American Indian life'—especially those that are not immediately visible: 'His plots are often based on highly sensitive aspects of Indian life that are likely to be ignored or denied by tribal traditionalists and academic purists.' "[3] The Methuen guide showcases only twenty-five playwrights between the sixties and the present. This puts him in the company of Edward Albee, Arthur Miller, Sarah Ruhl, and August Wilson, a personal hero to him.

All of this is undeniably true. One should not gather, however, that Bill's plays are pity parties, presenting the "plight" of the tragic Indian that whites so love because it permits them for an hour or two to feel guilty and sad and then shower and wash it all off. Bill Yellow Robe—in person, on the printed page, and most especially on stage—is hysterically funny. The plays anthologized here display the full gamut of his emotional palette. They range from tragedy to satire to flat-out farce. Even within the most realist and grim depictions, there is a leavening of Native humor. Such humor for Yellow Robe, as for Gerald Vizenor and Native people in general, is a key tool of survivance, Vizenor's neologism combining "survival" and "endurance." Yellow Robe writes to declare that his Assiniboine/Nakota people are still here—that Indians and Native nations are still here—and, despite fearful odds, have often thrived. He is an optimist, not a pessimist.

Yellow Robe was born and raised on the Fort Peck Indian Reservation in northeastern Montana. He wrote his first plays when he was in the sixth grade. (In a 2014 interview with the National Endowment for Arts for its *Art Works Blog*, he describes them as rip-offs of movies he had seen on television: the first was about Cleopatra, and the second was about the Twelve Labors of Hercules.)[4] He became involved in theater in junior high and high school. When he was in his mid-twenties, his parents asked if he was serious about being a playwright. When he said that he was, they both told him that then he had better leave Fort Peck because there was nothing for him on the reservation. He writes, "They were right. There were no professional theater companies, very few community theater productions, just the high-school drama productions. There was nothing to support me as a playwright, actor, or director."[5] He took their advice. Since then he has moved back and forth between the reservation and the outside world.

Not that the process has been always easy. He developed an alcohol problem (now long in the past). He lost his first wife to metastatic breast cancer. For three years, as he cared for her, he withdrew from playwriting. He taught at the Institute of American Indian Arts in Santa Fe, but was fired in 1996 when over half the faculty was let go because of a budget crisis.[6] In 1998, he was homeless and broke. He was conducting auditions for a production of *Waiting for Godot* he was directing, and it was not going well. He thought of giving up on the theater. At this low point in his life, he encountered a woman he had met as a reporter when he and the other Native faculty were let go. She went on to become his second wife and helped him put his life back together.[7]

Yellow Robe's plays often involve a return to home and tribal community and recognition that belonging is both a privilege and a responsibility. As Margo Lukens puts it, "The community system maintains the privilege of its membership, and when anyone questions it or threatens to break it down, those who have been comfortable within it naturally become fearful and angry."[8]

Another recurrent theme in Bill's work is mixed-blood identity and belonging. The plays selected by him and Lukens for *Grandchildren of the Buffalo Soldiers and Other Untold Stories* were chosen around this theme. In the title play of that collection, he tackles the issue of race. He himself is a descendant of one of those African American cavalrymen of the title.[9] It is an issue to which he periodically returns.

The plays we selected to be anthologized here are unified by supernatural themes or significant supernatural elements, hence the title *Restless Spirits*. Perhaps wanting to demonstrate that he was not limited to pure realism, the theme was Bill's suggestion, and it proved a felicitous one. Lukens writes, "The characters in Yellow Robe's plays are not simple, nor is his understanding of their situations throughout the play ever pat or formulaic. He shows the numerous aspects that make up one person—their guilt, their self-serving, their degree of maturity and their reflections on what they may have been or done in their youth, their flexibility or rigidity, the way they make sense of tribal tradition or history and use it to include or exclude people from their relationships."[10] He has said that one of his best-known and frequently performed plays, *Sneaky*, was a difficult one for him to write because all three brothers in the play represent different lives he had lived.[11] The spirits in these plays are indeed restless—haunted by unspeakable acts, by homophobia, by racism, by identity politics, by foreigners who invaded, stole their land, assaulted their culture and way of life. These are attacks that continue to this day.

This book brings together one full-length play and seven one-act plays. The two-act, *Wood Bones*, is a major work. It begins the volume. It had a recent successful production, which Yellow Robe directed, at the University of Maine, where he currently teaches. The anthology concludes with his most recent one-act, *One Step In*, a hilarious farce, which had a staged reading with Yellow Robe directing and acting at the Returning the Gift Literary Festival at the University of Oklahoma in 2017.

Wood Bones involves a house where horrific acts were committed. The house itself retains memories of them, as subsequent occupants discover.

In *Frog's Dance*, the deracinated mixed-blood nephew of the title character moves from the city to the reservation to live with his uncle. Initially resistant, he learns where he fits in and how to be an Indian. Throughout the play, Frog communes with the spirits of his dead sister and his wife, who was the love of his life. It is a touching and poignant piece.

In *Wink-Dah*, Death and the Trickster provide a humorous counterpoint to an earthly tragedy. A gay Indian youth is brutalized by the bigoted white father of his lover. This sets in motion a series of events that will destroy all three. (An example of the comic relief comes when Trickster challenges Death to a game for the fate of his friend; Death produces a chessboard, a clever reference to Ingmar Bergman's *The Seventh Seal*, presumably the last time Death played someone over a person's fate.)

Falling Distance involves two young lovers, separated from each other by different planes of existence. They will be reunited through the magic of a very special mirror.

To Cross takes place at the border between two worlds. It involves reincarnation, as the lead character makes the passage from the spirit world to ours with an ageless Indian as his guide. It tackles issues of identity and assimilation.

It Came from Across the Big Pond is inspired by 1950s science fiction films like *It Came from Outer Space* and *Invasion of the Body Snatchers*. It also bears a resemblance to Philip K. Dick's short story, "Adjustment Team." In it, the reservation is invaded by a team of "Assimilation Processors" who practice "social gentrification," turning Indians into whites.

Tiger Lily Two-Step is a satire of cultural appropriation and representation. Wannabe powwows are cursed by the appearance of a "little person," who turns out to be Tiger Lily, the leader of the Indians of Neverland in *Peter Pan*.

Finally, *One Step In* is a farce that deals with identity politics and those who wield them as a weapon against those they deem less "authentic" than themselves. It is set in the waiting room of heaven where a full-blood is having trouble gaining entry.

Yet another recurring theme in Bill Yellow Robe's work is tribal national sovereignty—territorial, economic, cultural—and those who defend it, manipulate it, or would extinguish it. In *It Came from Across the Big Pond*, one of the processors touts the benefit of assimilation, saying, "In a way, but you won't have all that difficult business of being sovereign. Something you people wanted long ago, and when a little of it was given to you there were so many problems created by it. Treaties, agreements—it was a huge legal mess. Now we have something new that will help you become better situated in our society." A few minutes later, evoking the cultural genocide of forced conversion and the boarding schools, he says, "We wanted you to be a part of us a long time ago. Your people were baptized, inducted, educated, cleaned up, but it didn't do a lot for your development of assimilation. These two new processes will help you regenerate a new interest and move the process along. It isn't going to be painful, a little difficult for her [a full-blood character], but we've designed this, again, specifically for your people."

His commitment to tribal sovereignty explains why, of all the numerous performances of his work—at New York's Public Theater, at literary festivals, in national tours, at Yale and other universities—the one that Yellow Robe is perhaps most proud was a production of *Sneaky* staged by Water Protectors at Oceti Sakowin Camp during the Standing Rock Sioux's standoff over the Dakota Access Pipeline crossing under the Missouri River. That protest was particularly significant to him because the Missouri flows near his home in Wolf Point on the Fort Peck Reservation.

Bill considers his plays the gift he has to give to Native communities and Native people. In the NEA interview, he states, "One of the things that really amazes me is that it has a tremendous healing element. It can heal an individual, it can heal a community, but it has to be set up so that there's a sense of security, trust, respect, and patience. And you know what's really the problem now is that, in my career with my plays, I've always been put in that position: am I doing this for community, or am I doing it for a career? And I've never seen my writing as a career; I've always seen it as a responsibility."¹² When performed in Native community, it might be an audience member's first experience of theater. Even if it was not, it was probably the first time they had seen people who looked and thought like them represented affirmatively and accurately on the stage. He says that when he staged his works in communities, people would inevitably ask him where they could get copies of the script to share with others. He began to carry photocopies of his plays with him, to give to those who asked—an expensive, and muscle-taxing, process. In his preface to the Lukens anthology, he writes that it is exciting for him to see his plays published and anthologized, writing, "It isn't for the sake of money, fame, or prestige; it is for the sake of helping the community."¹³ With this volume, they have access to eight previously unavailable plays—for those who have the wherewithal to purchase it.

Yellow Robe has been the recipient of numerous awards. Most recently he received the 2018 Lifetime Achievement Award from the Native Writers' Circle of the Americas.

If I may be permitted to end on a personal note, I must say that of all my projects this has been the most pleasurable and gratifying. Bill Yellow Robe has, in the process of editing this volume, become a dear personal friend. Already widely performed and studied, it is my hope that, if this volume is successful, it will lead to further collections of his work. After all, less than a third of his output has been anthologized and published.

I have deliberately kept this introduction brief. I want to permit Bill's words to shine on their own.

Wood Bones

Characters

121, a spirit of a home; timeless and ageless
LEROY, a Native man who helps 121
JACOB EAGLES, a young Native man
VERA EAGLES, a young Native woman, wife to Jacob
CHRISTEN, a troubled mother
SAM, a gravely troubled husband
MARY, daughter to Christen, a young girl of ten years
CALVIN, a Native worker, jack of all trades but master of none
NEIL, a newly discovered Native man and businessman
DOUG JENSEN, deputy sheriff
VERONICA PETERSON, a businessman and owner of property

Act One

SCENE ONE

LEROY, *an older man in his early fifties, stops to light a cigarette. He has an abalone shell with sage slowly smoldering at his feet.* 121, *dressed in a white suit appears and slowly walks toward* LEROY. 121 *smiles at* LEROY.

LEROY
Ho-lee! Uh, hello? How are you?

121
Get out. Get out! Get out!

LEROY
I am.

121
Yes. You are—out. And I'm . . .

LEROY
Still here.

121
Do I know you? I believe I've seen you before? Aren't you . . . ?

LEROY
No. We've never actually met. I've passed near here several times when I was just a kid. When we drove into town we would ride past you and just look at you. You were very pretty.

121
But not now?

LEROY
Well, time can be hard on all of us, some more than others, but a hard ride, uh, I'm not saying . . .

121
You don't have to. It is how I feel. I feel so—alone.

LEROY
Loneliness doesn't always need time to make you feel that way.

121
I haven't been alone?

LEROY
No. It was just a few years since, well, since the last time.

121
I'm sorry. Did you say who you are?

LEROY
No, but I'm Leroy Rose. I live south of town here, near the agency.

121
Hello, Leroy. I'm . . . I'm . . . my name is—was . . . did I say I was alone?

LEROY
Don't worry. It'll come to you.

121
I have a name—of course I do! Everybody and everything has a name. Mine is, uh, it is . . .

LEROY
Let me get back to work and it might come back to you.

121
Work? What are you doing?

LEROY
Helping you. All the different ones you've known in the past. I'm helping all of you. I'm completing something that didn't happen a long time ago.

121
What? Well, uh, well, that's good, I suppose. Can I help? What can I do to help you, Leroy?

LEROY
Just stand over there and when I finish, we'll talk.

121
Over there? Why don't I just go over here . . . ?

[*Tries to move and is met with a barrier.*]

What?

LEROY
Don't worry. It'll be gone. Then you can move. Just go and stand over there. You'll know when it's time.

121
Leroy? Hurry, please. I feel like things are changing. I can't stop them. I'm, I'm scared?

LEROY
If you feel like you are going. I'm here. Don't be afraid.

[*He puts down his cigarette and puts it out. He picks up the abalone shell. Lights fade.*]

SCENE TWO

Onstage, in a different area, are JACOB *and* VERA EAGLES. *They stand looking at* 121. JACOB *holds a bag of popcorn. They have just returned from the fair.*

VERA
That's worth a *lilili*. It's so huge! Who could buy something like that?

JACOB
When we started working on it, Peterson, the old man, he couldn't make it up the stairs. I had to carry everything, even him. Just like all Indians, we have to bear everything.

VERA
Oh, Jacob, don't tease! How much do you think it costs, Jacob?

JACOB
I don't know. I think Peterson is going to restore it and sell it. Veronica likes her money.

VERA
The people who owned it before must have had a big family.

JACOB
No. It was that old couple who moved here from Wyoming. Remember? He was part of a home settler family from a long time ago. Back when they used to fear us. Well, he left and then returned here to retire.

VERA
Why here?

JACOB
He started a family, like we are.

VERA
But not as fast as us, enit?

[*They both laugh.*]

What Indians have that kind of money?

JACOB
Me. And that means us.

VERA
I doubt it, Jacob.

JACOB
You never know, Vera. One day we could be holding the keys that open that front door. Wouldn't that be something?

VERA
Keys we can always have, but to provide for a family, that is something else.

JACOB
If we have more kids, would you want something like this to raise them in? Give them a good start in this world.

VERA
I don't need something like that to raise our kids.

JACOB
Oh. Something half the size of a box car, huh?

VERA
Oh—no! We're doing fine with what we have right now.

JACOB
Well, if we had something that size, other Indins would never believe Indins could live in something like that.

VERA
Yes. They would be accusing us of acting too good if we had something like that.

JACOB
The white people here would be burning crosses in our front yard—

VERA
Oh, not that bad! It isn't that way.

JACOB
Sometimes it feels that way. When I was working at the other job in the mill they didn't know I was an Indian. They kept asking me if I were a Mexican, or part colored. I told them I was Indian they said, "Oh, one of our Indians."

VERA
That's because we aren't on the reservation.

JACOB
We are. Yeah, we're a long mile away. This is all Indian land. But one day we'll get this land back.

   [121 *waves at them.*]

VERA
Jacob! Did you see that?

JACOB
See what?

VERA
Is there somebody in that house?

JACOB
No. Why? What did you see?

VERA
I thought I saw someone wave at me.

JACOB
What?

VERA
Right there. I thought I saw something move.

JACOB
Wait, point with your finger this time, not your lips.

VERA
Oh, Jacob.

JACOB
You probably saw a tree branch reflecting from the windows. There's no one there.

VERA
Are you sure?

JACOB
Yeah. Hey, we'd better get back to the apartment. Your mom's cooking tonight and she wants to make sure everybody is there when she sets her table.

VERA
I feel sorry for her. Who knew Andrew would do that?

JACOB
I enlisted when I was his age. Graduated from boarding school and right into service, the ink was still wet on my diploma.

VERA
Have you ever heard of that place he went to?

JACOB
No, but no one heard of the place I went to when I was sent away. My mom kept on asking me where they were sending me. After my first tour I had to finally get a map and show her where Korea was.

VERA
You know what, Jacob? It does look nice.

JACOB
Looks nice, but we'll make it look better, like a home. Let's see if the old man's daughter will give it up.

Blackout. End of scene

SCENE THREE

Lights up on two men. They are taking a break. They are local men, not construction workers, but handymen. They see LEROY *holding a lit braid of sweet grass and smudging the area around them.*

NEIL
Jesus Christ. What the hell is that old Indian doing? Not one of your relations is it, Cal?

CALVIN
No. Looks like Solomon Tails, but he's not around. I wonder why he's doing that.

NEIL
Keeping his mojo working, I suppose. We are in the twentieth century. Hell, I thought you people were civilized, Cal?

CALVIN
I am. I don't believe in that shit. Hey! Sol'!

NEIL
No. Let him finish. It won't hurt us.

CALVIN
Hey—ah, Neil. Do you believe those stories? You know—the ones about this place?

NEIL
What? Hell no. Calvin, did you load those stain glass windows from downstairs yet?

CALVIN
Yeah. Where are you going to take them to get them fixed?

NEIL
No place around here. I'll have to drive up to Fargo. There's a guy who does the windows for the churches. He'll take a look at them. Did you get the broken pieces, as well?

CALVIN
Yeah. All of it loaded in a box in the back of your truck.

NEIL
The old house door is made of solid oak. Did you see it?

CALVIN
Yeah. It weighs a ton.

NEIL
Those stupid-ass kids who were renting here couldn't close the door, so they took it off the hinges and sanded it and then took a saw to it—made it lopsided as hell.

CALVIN
No way.

NEIL
Yeah. One of them was a student at the vo-tech and he was the one who did it. What a dumb ass. Maybe he was learning to be a baker. Sure the hell wasn't a carpenter.

CALVIN
Too bad. I don't know if we'll be able to fix it.

NEIL
Did you see the frames? They stuck so much goop for insulation you can't fit a "standard" door in it.

CALVIN
I notice they cut the ropes inside the window frame, as well.

NEIL
Yeah. Those are old-time windows with the weights. You don't see those around here. There are a couple of houses that have them, but white families take care of their homes.

CALVIN
How many people were staying here? I'm still bagging trash from upstairs.

NEIL
It was clean once, a long, long time ago. . . .

CALVIN
It looks like they were burning candles in one of the bedrooms. There's wax all over the window sill.

NEIL
I'm just thankful they weren't sniffing paint or glue.

CALVIN
I heard this was a big party house—"pass-out palace."

NEIL
Yep. All the gifts of "affirmative action." Load up those floorboard frames. I'll fix them at my house.

CALVIN
That's some nice wood.

NEIL
We'll have to replaster the bathroom wall upstairs . . .

CALVIN
There must have been three families in here at once.

NEIL
No. There was one girl and her friends. At one time she had sixteen people living in here.

CALVIN
No one said anything?

NEIL
If it were me, they'd be tossed out. I remember hearing that. The Behrs used to own this house back in the late forties. They would rent rooms out to farm kids who came in after harvest to go to school. The kids and the family took care of the house. The girl who was renting it recently turned this into a major party house. In the late mornings you could walk by the house and look into the window and see a great peep show. Some people said the shows were better than what was on cable.

CALVIN
Are you going to rebuild or replace the banisters?

NEIL
Yeah. I still have to get those two-inch screws out of the upstairs hallway floors as well . . .

121
Where are—my—

CALVIN
Did you hear that?

NEIL
It's the house.

121
Shhhh-t! That hurts!

CALVIN
Still settling? How old is this place?

NEIL
Oh Christ, don't get scared.

CALVIN
But you heard that, right? Neil?

NEIL
You know what, Calvin? I'm starting to think you're trying to get out of work early today.

CALVIN
What? No. That's bullshit!

121
Who—who are you?

NEIL
I heard that, too.

CALVIN
What is that? An owl?

NEIL
Ignore it! This house is pretty beat up. It could be anything from upstairs. You saw the walls and the ceiling.

CALVIN
That sounded—sounded like it was all around us. Are we here by ourselves?

NEIL
I'm the only one who has the keys. The police told each of those kids to stay away from this house. I've changed all the locks. Unless they broke the windows . . .

CALVIN
Well, the back porch has no window and just a piece of chain link for a door.

[*He exits.*]

NEIL
Calvin? Hey! Come here.

[CALVIN *returns*.]

CALVIN
There's nothing back there.

NEIL
What'd I say? I told you we're the only ones here.

CALVIN
It just didn't sound like, you know, like a house noise.

NEIL
Look. I'll give you something for your work . . .

[*Begins to take his wallet out and counts out some money.*]

CALVIN
I said I heard something, Neil!

121
I—I—

CALVIN
Well, if that was a house sound, what was that, then?

NEIL
It sounds the same as before. I didn't hear anything different.

CALVIN
Are you going to live here after you fix it up?

NEIL
No. I'm going to sell it again. It's going to take a lot of work. I'll stay here at night if I have to. No one is going to torch this after all the work I've put into it.

CALVIN
Yeah, but a lot of stuff happened in this house over the years.

NEIL
Old stories! There's no truth in them. Like a bunch of damn scared kids. Some noise in the night and people believe this place is haunted, cursed, some made up, make-believe bullshit.

CALVIN
Then why are you tearing it down?

NEIL
I'm not. I'm just taking out the rotted stuff. A lot of the wood has been left to rot. Instead of grafting, I'm going to amputate this sucker. Hell, the Tribe finally bought this tract back and whether the Tribal Government knows it or not this land is a good lot.

121
B-ace . . .

NEIL
Hear that? It sounds really loud, and then went soft.

CALVIN
You heard it? Really? What did it sound like? Sounded kinda human, huh?

NEIL
Come here. It sounded like this . . .

[*He does a raspberry into* CALVIN's *ear.*]

CALVIN
You son of a . . .

NEIL
What happened to the warrior? Stop crying! Jesus! Let's get this done, or you'll be working for that old man out there.

Lights slowly fade out on CALVIN *and* NEIL.

SCENE FOUR

In the center stage, lights come up on a young couple, an Indian man and a white woman. We go back several years. The man and woman are SAM *and* CHRISTEN.

CHRISTEN
I can't believe it. We can buy this place.

SAM
We'll finally have a home, Christen baby. The home you've always wanted baby. No more welfare hotels for my baby girl.

CHRISTEN
We can fix it up real nice and when we get tired of it we can sell it and make our money back, including extra.

SAM
You mean this isn't your "little house on the rez" house you've always wanted?

CHRISTEN
What? Pa, don't tease me like that. That's mean. As long as I have you and Mary I would be happy anywhere. And this house will be the new member of our family. Anyways.

SAM
Really, my baby girl? Do I make you that happy?

CHRISTEN
You sure do, Poppa.

SAM
Then do me a favor, my sweet baby. The next time I have to go to the agency to meet with the Tribal Loans Department, keep your daughter at home with your mom. I don't want any of the council members to see her. When she walks around everybody stares at her, and she causes a big distraction. And, I know this is hard, but I don't want them thinking she's mine.

CHRISTEN
Don't say things like that, Sam. She is my—our daughter. You said her hair is so pretty. I've heard you tell her that myself.

SAM
Yeah, but you have to understand. It isn't me. It's those other people. They'll see her as being part nigger. I'm an Indin. It has been hard enough for people around here to see me as an Indian and not a person who is black. Remember, Christen. I love you, but I'm not some minority, and I'm not some goddamn nigger!

CHRISTEN
Don't say that word. I've never seen you or her in any way but as my family. She can't help it. Why would you use that word? Who taught you to say that word? Not me!

SAM
Your mother and her people for a start. And some of these other white people around here, but they call me a "prairie nigger." The next time you can just leave her at your mom's!

CHRISTEN
Are you saying you don't want her living with us? Sam? That's so silly to get hung up on that. Don't say something that is so mean, honey . . .

SAM
No. I'm saying the next time we have business with the Tribes, you leave her at your mother's and this is the last time I'll ever say it. I promise you. You see how they look at us when we walk through the Tribal buildings? There she is, dark as a piece of coal, me, light brown like toast, and you, white as Space Ghost. No. I don't mean it that bad, but you see what I mean.

CHRISTEN
No. I don't because it was never easy for me. I've raised her by myself, and no one ever offered to . . .

SAM
Yes! I know! I've heard this, but you aren't alone any more, are you? Look at me, baby girl. I married you, and you came with a family. I'm not

complaining, but I want to make sure you and your little girl—our baby girl, Mary, is safe here. That's all I'm doing is watching out for us. Help me do this, honey, baby girl. We have a beautiful house now, for my beautiful family. Now, go and bring her in. She can have her own room.

[CHRISTEN *exits.* SAM *does some business.* CHRISTEN *enters with her daughter* MARY.]

CHRISTEN
Did you want me to go to the store and get something for supper tonight? We should have something special to celebrate.

SAM
Yes. You got money?

CHRISTEN
No.

SAM
Of course, I'm the husband, the provider. Here, I have money for our celebration my lovely white squaw.

[*He removes his wallet and hands her some bills.*]

CHRISTEN
I'm going to get something special for Mary.

SAM
Wow, that is so cool Christen. You watch out for that little girl the way other Indian women do. That is so cool.

CHRISTEN
Sam, thank you. That is so sweet. Makes up for the "squaw" smart-ass remark.

SAM
Yeah. Go and get us something real "goot"!

CHRISTEN
I'll be right back, Pa.

SAM
Don't worry and rush back because we aren't going anywhere. We have finally found a home.

[*Lights change and we see* MARY *in her new room. She is slowly walking around. She goes to a window and looks out.* 121 *slowly enters the room.* MARY *quickly turns and sees no one.*]

MARY
Hello?

[121 *waves at* MARY, *but is unseen by her.*]

Who's there?

[*She slowly walks around the room.*]

Hello?

[121 *reaches out to* MARY, *nearly touching her.*]

You don't scare me.

[121 *backs away.*]

Is that what you're trying to do? If someone is in here, come out! All right, if you don't come out. Show me you are here.

[121 *moves a toy but all* MARY *sees is the toy move.*]

What! No, oh no, no, that is so cool! If you are here, could you please do that again?

[121 *moves the toy again.*]

Who are you? Hello? Are you a ghost? Like Casper? You are not a demon or a devil, are you? If you are, you'd better leave—right now! If you are a ghost, like a friendly ghost. You can stay with me.

[*Sounds of somebody coming up the stairs can be heard.*]

SAM
Who the hell are you talking to?

[*He enters the room. 121 backs away.*]

MARY
No one?

SAM
No one, huh? That's what I am? Just joshing you. Well, you like your room?

MARY
It's so cool, Pa. I really love it. I can't wait to have my friends here to play.

SAM
First step is, here, I brought you your blankets.

[*He holds one of the black garbage sacks.*]

We'll get you a bed later on. For now, you'll have to sleep on the floor.

MARY
You mean I'll get a bed, too?

SAM
Not now, but maybe later. Here. Take these.

[*She slowly approaches him and takes the bag.*]

What's wrong with you?

MARY
Nothing. I don't want to play now.

SAM
Do you think I would be bad to my little sweetie, do you?

MARY
No. I just thought since I've been so good I would get a bed.

SAM
You sound just like your mother. That's why I can't play games like we do with her, because she always wants expensive nice things. It can really make me feel sad. I didn't hurt you the last time we played, did I?

MARY
Yes. No! I mean, no, Pa.

SAM
When you get hurt from our playing, what do you tell people?

MARY
That, I was careless, and fell off my bike. It's my own fault.

SAM
Good. You keep saying that. I'll make sure you will always have a bike.

[*He begins to leave.*]

121
Alone . . . Leave her alone!

MARY
What was that?

SAM
House settling. Get your bed made. We'll eat when your mom gets back.

[SAM *stops at the door and watches* MARY *take blankets out of the bag and lay them on the floor.* SAM *slowly closes the bedroom door, while still in the room.*]

MARY
Please don't leave me. "*Kona, we-ah,*" that's what my friends at school say. I'm a "*we-ah.*" I hope you are, too. Please be my, "*kona.*"

[121 *covers her mouth.*]

Blackout. End of scene.

SCENE FIVE

Lights up in the same area as the beginning of the play. LEROY *sits on the ground, gathering a few items he has placed on the ground.* 121 *enters and cautiously approaches him.*

121
I know you.

LEROY
Hau', how are you? You've come back, Sis. I'm nearly done.

121
Done? What were you doing?

LEROY
Getting things ready for one more round. Then I'm going home.

121
Where is your home?

LEROY
I live at the agency, a few miles that a way.

121
You've pointed with your lips.

LEROY
Yes.

121
I've seen that done before. I can't remember—I—I think—wasn't it you?

LEROY
Might've been, I suppose. It could have been a long time ago, or a few days ago.

121
We've—we had a conversation, or talked, before, right?

LEROY
Yes. It was earlier today. Now.

121
You're an Indian? An American Indian, aren't you?

LEROY
Sure hope so. Scare my grandparents if I weren't.

121
And, and there is something else. I can see it. I've never seen this before in a, uh—

LEROY
Indin?

121
A person.

LEROY
Same thing.

121
Yes, but when I look at a person I see one thing, or another. A slight glowing of shadows of themselves, male or female, but with you I see both shadows. Not overlapping one another, but living side-by-side.

LEROY
Does that bother you? I'm what we called "two spirit."

121
Could I be "two spirit"?

LEROY
You have been many things, but when we are finished here, you'll know.

121
Could I have been an American Indian?

LEROY
You could've been, I don't know.

121
There were only two kinds, two kinds, of people here?

LEROY
Depends on whose eyes your looking through, but there are three, counting the animals, and still more.

121
I wouldn't know about that. I just knew of two kinds of people. The Indians and the Christians.

LEROY
White, they used to call themselves the homesteaders. Settled the west.

121
What?

LEROY
Most of the people you knew were probably *wacijus*, or white, and Christians.

121
Are Indians Christians, too?

LEROY
Some of them are. Yes.

121
I had white skin at one time, not always. Maybe I'm white? With blue arms?

LEROY
Now, take it easy. Besides, I wouldn't know the answer to that.

121
I'm white, American Indian, Christian, and if I'm part "animal"—maybe bird? No wonder I'm so confused.

LEROY
It happens that way sometimes, to a lot of us. I'm going home to get something to eat. It's past one, but I'll be back later. I'll be finished before the sun goes down.

121
All right. I'll be right here.

LEROY
Not for long, if I do this right.

[*He begins to exit.*]

Lights fade. Blackout. End of scene.

SCENE SIX

Lights up and it is CHRISTEN *and* SAM *sitting on some metal folding chairs.* SAM *is smoking a cigarette.* CHRISTEN *is looking through the local newspaper.*

SAM
You get any bites yet?

CHRISTEN
No. There's nothing here in town. If you don't work for the Tribes or agency there is nothing. There is a job for a cashier at the Center Gas Station in Saco, but that would be a thirty-mile drive back and forth.

SAM
Our car might blow up before you see your first paycheck. How much are they paying?

CHRISTEN
Big time, eight dollars an hour.

SAM
That's more than I ever get.

CHRISTEN
I could get a job at Sinclair here in town. It doesn't pay eight dollars an hour and it isn't full time. They have an ad for a night shift person. From six to eleven. No medical or other benefits.

SAM
I'm your old man. Because of that my Tribe will allow you to get medical and dental work. I guess that's one benefit in being with me, huh?

CHRISTEN
No, Mary. She needs to see a doctor.

SAM
Why? Why would she need to see a doctor? Is she sick?

CHRISTEN
She'll need a physical when she starts school.

SAM
I thought you were going to homeschool her? It'll be better than what she'll get at that damn public school. And don't forget how these kids are around here. They see she's black, and they'll take after her for it. These kids don't know how to act.

CHRISTEN
Sam, why don't you count her as your own daughter? She could get medical and free education . . .

SAM
Think about that for a minute, baby girl. Look what we went through when we were dating? The attitudes we got when we went to the Tribal Building. If we try to do the paper work on Mary, imagine all the dirt people will dig up and throw at us for having her. That's a lot of pressure we can do without.

CHRISTEN
Do you really think it will be that bad, Sam?

SAM
Look it, we'll have to tell them who her real dad is. You'll have to explain to the members of the enrollment committee how you went out for a party one night, met a black guy, had a party with him, got "knocked up," and that's how they'll word it, and gave birth to this girl that the real father doesn't care for, or probably doesn't know.

CHRISTEN
It was an accident, but the truth is, it became the best thing in my life. I had Mary. They really won't go into all these details in the committee, will they? That would be horrible if we had to go through all that just to get her medical . . .

SAM
It'll be far worse. It just won't stay in the committee, but the committee members will be on the phones later and spread this information around the agency, then the rez, then the white communities. So much for professionalism.

CHRISTEN
She will have to start school. She'll be in the sixth grade. She will need a medical checkup. She hasn't had one in a long time.

SAM
Well, when you get your job and I start working, we'll pull our money together and take her to a real medical doctor, not this Indian Health Service. I don't think they have a doctor on staff right now. The nurses are playing doctors now.

CHRISTEN
I thought we still had money left after we bought the house? You said the loan would take care of the house, and we would have some money left over, so why can't we use a little bit of that money to have Mary examined?

SAM
Is she sick? Are you telling me everything? What's going on, Christen? Baby girl, you can tell me. Don't be afraid to come to me. I'm your husband.

121
No . . . listen . . . no . . .

CHRISTEN
What?

SAM
Didn't you hear what I said? I'm saying don't be afraid to come to me.

CHRISTEN
Yeah, but I heard something. Just as you were finishing what you were saying I thought I heard—oh, nothing. No. There is nothing wrong with Mary. Why are you so jumpy about this? Is it money?

121
Listen.

SAM
Well, I don't feel proud admitting it, but in a way it is. I mean, we were living in a monthly motel not long ago, and now I ran into some good luck and got a loan from the Tribe to improve my life, your life, our lives.

CHRISTEN
Wait! What?

SAM
Christen, I'm saying we now have a place we can call our own. We've gone a long time with little or no money. You know how hard it has been for me to find a job. People around here don't want to hire an Indian because of how they see us, especially when they are white and broke.

CHRISTEN
Yeah. I know that Sam, but I'm scared, too. I've been concerned thinking about what happens if Mary gets real sick. How will we take care of her?

SAM
What? Don't you worry about that, baby girl. I'm here. I'm her daddy, and I'll find a way to take care of her. Just like I found us a home. I can do this, Christen.

CHRISTEN
All right. Thank you, Poppa. Thank you.

SAM
Where is that kid, anyway?

CHRISTEN
She's in her room. I think she's playing.

SAM
Let's go out and get some grub?

CHRISTEN
I'll get her down. Mary!

[CHRISTEN *stands and takes a few steps.*]

Mary! Come downstairs baby.

[*There are sounds of movement.*]

121
Bye.
[MARY *slowly enters the room.*]

MARY
Yes, Mommy?

CHRISTEN
Guess what, baby? Daddy's taking us out for lunch. Are you hungry?

SAM
Whoa! What the hell is wrong with her hair!

CHRISTEN
She showered this morning. Her hair gets frizzy—

SAM
Better fix it. Christ, I'm not going into the café with her hair like that. People will stare at us. Looks like she came right from the fields.

CHRISTEN
I will, I will. Mary, baby, get Mommy's brush. I'll comb your hair.

[MARY *goes to one of the garbage bags and digs for a brush.*]

SAM
I can't imagine what these people will say. Maybe we should just go to the drive up.

CHRISTEN
No. I'll fix her hair. It won't be long. Come here, baby. Come sit here. Poppa is going to take us to the café for lunch. You can get a cheeseburger and tater tots. You like tater tots, momma's baby? The round fat french fries?

MARY
Uh-huh.

CHRISTEN
Then we'll come back and take a nap and maybe later we'll go play at the park. Would you like that?

MARY
Yes.

[CHRISTEN *starts to brush* MARY's *hair, but it is a painful process.*]

Ow.

CHRISTEN
I know it hurts, and I'm sorry, Mary. We should have done this right after your shower this morning.

MARY
Ow! Mommy, please don't pull my hair.

SAM
This is a lot just to brush some hair. Indian kids don't have this problem when they brush their hair.

CHRISTEN
Her hair is different.

SAM
Colored hair. Here. I'll hold her, and you brush it.

[SAM *walks over and holds* MARY's *arms, facing* MARY.]

CHRISTEN
All right, but be gentle.

MARY
No. I'll sit still. I'll be good.

SAM
Just be quiet. You're making too much noise. Go ahead. I have her.

CHRISTEN
It won't take long, Mary. Just be still.

[*She starts brushing* MARY's *hair again.*]

MARY
Ow.

CHRISTEN
It's all right. It won't take long.

MARY
Ow!

CHRISTEN
I'm being gentle as I can, baby.

[SAM *is smiling.*]

MARY
Ow!

[SAM *starts to laugh.*]

Blackout. End of scene.

SCENE SEVEN

Lights up on a different area of the stage, and we have NEIL *and* CALVIN. *They are wearing protective goggles and are covered in dirt and dust.*

CALVIN
Hey, Neil? Why is it they complain about the Tribe having a casino and a mega-gas station, but when all these white farmers north of us had that big oil boom and the big money, nobody says jack.

NEIL
They deserve it.

CALVIN
What?

NEIL
Yeah. They were wheat farmers, some cattlemen, and all of them were nearly broke. Then they got lucky and some oil company found mucho oil wells on their land, and now they are the Clampetts of the prairie.

CALVIN
We were like that a year ago.

NEIL
Yeah, but it's not the same. You Indians never worked before.

CALVIN
Where? Doing what?

NEIL
My point.

CALVIN
There isn't any work, but only in the summer and nothing for the rest of the year.

NEIL
You're getting in over your head, Calvin.

CALVIN
In bullshit, maybe.

NEIL
Hey, I'm your "cuh-zin." I wouldn't bullshit you.

CALVIN
Yeah, you became a real close relative after the Tribal Loan Committee cosigned your loan to buy this house.

NEIL
Are you mad? What the hell's your problem? I've always taken care of business. Remember, I couldn't make the tribal enrollment my first time, but giving the right gifts to the right people I was Indian enough.

CALVIN
By a nose bleed, don't have a nose bleed, Neil.

NEIL
I'll give you a nose bleed! Look, Calvin, if you're so upset, why are you even working with me? You can go work for housing, or roads.

CALVIN
Whoa, settle down Walks with Big Bucks! Lower them horns! How much did you pay for this place anyway?

NEIL
It wasn't much. About ten thousand. It was on the market for five years.

CALVIN
Nobody would touch it, huh?

NEIL
Nobody had the cash. All those farmers used to have two houses. One that was out in the boondocks for when they were planting and haying. The other one was for when they finished harvesting and had to come into town, so their kids could go to school. There are still about twenty of them on the market. If you want, when we finish this one, I'll help you do the paperwork so you can get yourself one.

CALVIN
I don't know. To leave that spacious wonderful cinderblock, cement floor, prefab HUD house would be hard to do.

121
Hurt?

CALVIN
For an old house this place makes a lot of noise, enit?

NEIL
Ignore that shit! You know, this place was built around the twenties. All of it was handcrafted wood. Too bad they didn't hang on to the furniture. Those old cherry wood cabinets, man. They would be worth a lot of money today.

CALVIN
Still, it's kind of creepy, you know?

NEIL
We can ask that old guy outside and to come in here and smoke this place if you get too scared.

CALVIN
Hey—

NEIL
What?

CALVIN
How long have we been working?

NEIL
Why? Are you tired? This little break is all I need.

CALVIN
No. I'm not tired, but it's like we've been working all morning long, and I'm not hungry. You?

NEIL
My wife always makes a good farmer's breakfast.

CALVIN
Spam and eggs?

NEIL
No. Big O-steak, T-bone, with four scrambled eggs and some fried potatoes with chopped red onions. A few pieces of toast, buttered with grape jelly, and a big glass of milk.

CALVIN
What, no biscuits and gravy? No OJ?

NEIL
Better than what you have, I bet. What was it? Deer rib soup and a four-day-old piece of frybread?

CALVIN
Make you jealous, huh? But you're not hungry, huh?

NEIL
I have a paper sack around here with some sandwiches and some pop, if you want a sandwich.

CALVIN
No. I'm just saying it seems like we've been working for a long damn time.

121
In-In-inn . . .

CALVIN
Did you hear that?

NEIL
Yeah. It sounds like the wood frame I had leaning against the wall slid down and fell.

CALVIN
It sounds like it came from her room.

NEIL
What?

CALVIN
You know. The little girl had a room on the second floor.

NEIL
Next to the room with guy with the hook for a hand?

CALVIN
Don't be such a smart ass, Neil. You know what I'm talking about.

NEIL
No. I don't.

CALVIN
The people who had this house before.

NEIL
A lot of people owned this house, rented this house—hell, probably squatted in this house for so many years. This house is half the age of the state. It has a history. What little girl are you talking about in particular?

CALVIN
You know. The one. Five years ago. The Indin guy, his white wife, and the girl? That one.

NEIL
Oh, Jesus Christ. Which "one"?

CALVIN
Never mind. You don't believe in these things anyway.

NEIL
There are so many stories about these houses, Calvin. Every damn one of them. If you believe all these stories no one would be buying or trying to live in these houses. The way Indins around here talk about spirits and stuff, you would be scared to even step into a yard without causing some trouble or violating some spirit. Get a grip on yourself. What you heard upstairs was a wood frame from the window that I took off, put up alongside the

wall, and it slid and fell. That's all. There aren't any spirits, spooks, or shit like that in this house.

CALVIN
Sorry I said anything.

NEIL
Find that paper sack of food. Maybe you're hungry and that's what's making you so jumpy.

CALVIN
What kind of sandwiches did you bring?

NEIL
Some roast beef we had the night before. A lot of mustard and pepper on them.

CALVIN
Yeah. Maybe I'll eat later.

NEIL
Eat now.

CALVIN
I said I'm all right.

NEIL
This is the last time we do this. Are you sure you want to get one of these houses? If you're so damn sensitive about the noises.

CALVIN
Don't get so bossy, Neil. I said I'm all right. You always have to go overboard when somebody says something.

NEIL
Good. Buck up. Now, later on this afternoon I want to put in that oil tank I bought. We'll put it in to replace the chimneys. I'm going to close those off, so we can heat this place with oil. I don't want electric because it'll be expensive this fall.

CALVIN
All right.

121
Hur—t.

CALVIN
So, there are two window frames you have up against the wall?

Lights fade. Blackout. End of scene.

SCENE EIGHT

Lights up on 121. *She is standing in the same area where she met* LEROY. *She is looking around.*

121
Hello? Hello?

   [*Chirps.*]

I'm here. Wherever here is? Wait. Uh, I knew he told me his name. He said his name is Lucy? Leon? No, it was, Roy? No. It is Leroy. He is an American Indian. This is good. I'm getting to make all of this connect. Now. He went to get something to eat. That way?

   [*She points with her lip.*]

I wonder if I should eat? Do I eat? Is there a time to eat? I'm so confused. I wish he were here. He might know. I hate when things are this scattered. I was never this separated from my, my, things—myself. I don't like this. I wish somebody were here. I wish he were here. I feel so—so—old? Not like the rocks and trees, not that important, to life I mean, but young. I was so young at one time. I wasn't brought here. I was—I was given life here! Yes. That is one thing I can remember. I'm from here. There are so many things that are fading to me, and some things that I have inside of me that make me feel so weak, like I'm crumbling. Memories build, and just when I can touch them, they fade, crumble. I can nearly feel them on my fingertips, and just when I can form my fingers around one of them, they just disappear. Maybe this is what getting old is.

I can remember these things inside of me. I remember the things that would tickle inside of me. Laughter—yes! Laughter was one of the things. It starts like a short burst of electricity and lingers inside of me. It races all through me. It comes from the darkness and brings life to the inside of me, like rain. It is an amazing thing. The warmth it brings. It touches all parts of me. I miss you. Then there is the other type of laughter. Laughter that is cruel and mean. I could never understand how laughter could cause two types of feelings within me. This other laughter comes from a field of white hate. It wouldn't start there, but it would take me there. Anger, anger moves to rage, and then to a place of such hatred. It enflames the inside of me and I feel white and barren, like ash. It pushes everything out of me. There were only a few moments when I felt this. They linger in me just as long as the good laughter.

[*She tries to leave the area and is stopped abruptly.*]

What is that? Why am I here? LeRoy, I want to leave here. Even if I don't want something to eat, I should be allowed to leave. What is going on here?

[*Makes another attempt.*]

That feels so strong. Like a northern wind. I remember how the wind would come and brush up against me. It holds me. Some would say it is so cold, but it is so powerful. I feel at times if it wanted to pick me up and take me away it could. It didn't. It just held me. When the clouds changed, and they became dark with power, that wind became their equal. I remember seeing that wind. It took others and lifted them into the sky. I didn't think it was possible, but it is a power I respect, but never feared.

[*Makes another attempt.*]

Are you, you know, wind? Is that who you are? I would like to—to—move. Could you please allow me to move?

[*She has a sharp pain.*]

Oh. Oh. What is this? I've never felt that pain in the many years I've been here. You didn't cause that, did you?

[*Another pain.*]

Make it stop. It hurts. Please. Help me.

[*Lights fade on 121. She is now on the ground holding her side.*]

Blackout. End of scene.

SCENE NINE

Lights up on another part of the stage and we see NEIL *and* CALVIN. NEIL *is cutting some wood as* CALVIN *picks up the cut pieces.*

CALVIN
Are you nuts?

NEIL
I'll use this to replace the wood on the steps.

CALVIN
But what are you going to replace the wood along the sidings of the staircase with?

NEIL
I don't know, pine, maybe. I'll worry about it when the time comes. This will replace all those boards that are cut up and tore up. I don't know what those kids were doing. It looks like they were cutting into it with a hatchet, or an ax.

CALVIN
Probably to burn in the fireplace. I see they were burning trash in the fireplace.

NEIL
Too lazy to bag it and put it outside. I'm glad they didn't have an oil furnace here when that teenage girl was renting this place. They might have blown the whole damn house up.

CALVIN
How much more, Neil?

NEIL
What?

CALVIN
How much more do we have left to do today?

NEIL
As my dad says, "When you are done with that, then do that, and when you get that done, you could go and do this. If you get tired you can take a break, but make sure you do this while you're sitting down so it will get done."

CALVIN
I was just asking.

NEIL
Well, we cleared out all the crap from the attic.

CALVIN
Yeah, I did that. I got all that crap in bags and ready to go to the dump.

NEIL
Literally.

CALVIN
What?

NEIL
When that teenager rented this place, she had two guys renting the attic and sometimes when they partied too heavy, they couldn't make it down to the second floor.

CALVIN
Oh, Christ! I thought they had some dogs up there. Thanks for warning me.

NEIL
It was old. You should always wear gloves. Come on.

CALVIN
Oh, ten thousand for this honey of a home.

NEIL
Part of the house payment goes to paying for the court costs of that woman with the husband who was attacking her daughter.

CALVIN
See! You do know about the girl.

NEIL
Who doesn't? Poor little girl.

CALVIN
Is he still in the can?

NEIL
I guess. I don't know all the details. I'm not Paul Harvey.

CALVIN
Aren't they supposed to tell you all the history of the house when you buy it?

NEIL
Sometimes, but I wasn't interested in it.

CALVIN
But once you restore it, you are going to sell it again, aren't you? You'll have to tell the history of this house to whoever buys it, won't you? You will, won't you?

NEIL
If they ask, I might. I'm no storyteller and I'm too young to be a grandpa.

CALVIN
I'm glad you are not an elder. I was wondering if we should get rid of those pipes from the old steam heaters?

NEIL
Just leave them there and I'll take them over to Grandy's later on. They're always looking for scrap metals. We did what we could on the second floor. Just get the oil tank downstairs in place and we can call it a day.

CALVIN
I've noticed you been taking a lot out of the house. You aren't really interested in the restoration of this house, are you, Neil?

NEIL
Have you ever restored a house before?

CALVIN
Didn't see my sign, huh?

NEIL
So how would you know?

CALVIN
We've taken out a lot of good things that belong to this house, Neil. Those stain glass windows that weren't broken could have stayed where they were.

NEIL
I told you, I'm going to replace them with weatherized window frames and windows.

CALVIN
We've taken a lot of metal out of the walls and basement.

NEIL
Yeah.

CALVIN
You aren't going to restore this place like you said in your loan. You're going to strip it down and fix it up for renters, aren't you?

NEIL
Hey, people need a place to live. I'm just giving a helping hand to the community. Don't get me wrong. It would have been nice to restore this

old place, but people need a place to live. I figure I can get two or three separate apartments out of this house.

CALVIN
How much are you going to charge for rent?

NEIL
It will be a little more expensive since we've made all these repairs. Don't forget when we quit today, we'll have to come back in a few days, after that wood order comes in from Billings. We'll have a lot of new things in here.

CALVIN
A slum lord, Neil? Mighty urban of you.

NEIL
Shut the hell up. At least you're going to get paid. I won't see a damn cent until I place it on the market for renters.

CALVIN
Wow, tough there, Neil. How did you make out with the things you've taken from the house already?

NEIL
There were some nice things, but not big items. A few hundred, couple of thousand, here and there.

CALVIN
Doesn't this change your loan with the Tribes?

NEIL
Long as they don't know.

121
Where is it?

CALVIN
Did you hear that?

NEIL
How will the Tribe know? I'm not saying putting anything out there on the moccasin telegraph.

CALVIN
That sounded like it came from the second floor.

NEIL
How could it? There's no one up there. Ignore it.

CALVIN
But that's where that little girl was.

NEIL
It can't be a ghost, because she didn't die, remember?

CALVIN
How do you know?

NEIL
The copy of the police report I got from the realtor's office didn't mention it. They said she just disappeared.

CALVIN
Couldn't find the body. Yeah, because she's a ghost! See, I told you.

NEIL
That's not true. That's a story the old housewives tell one another. They found her. She was hiding up there somewhere on the second floor. They don't know how she got away, but she did. I heard she's living in Great Falls now. They put her in a foster home, and she is alive and well.

CALVIN
I don't like going up there. I don't want to work up there anymore. You can do it.

NEIL
Don't have to! Tomorrow we can come by and start loading the trash bags and make some runs to the city dump. I have a permit to dump. Then we can see to about painting the trim of the house.

121
Find it.

CALVIN
Maybe you shouldn't rent this place, Neil. It's already occupied.

Lights fade. Blackout. End of scene.

SCENE TEN

VERA *approaches* JACOB *who is resting by leaning on a shovel.*

JACOB
Are you all right Vera? Is there anything wrong?

[121 *stand in the background.*]

VERA
No. I just came to visit you. I thought you would be having lunch about now. I brought you some lunch.

[*He takes her hand and she holds a brown shoebox.*]

JACOB
I usually don't eat a lunch. His daughter threatens workers by deducting a lunch break from their pay. Are you sure everything is all right?

VERA
Yes. Everything is fine, Jacob. I finished all the laundry early this morning at the hotel, so the manager let me have a little extra time for my lunch. I was hoping he would, so I made this lunch before you got up.

JACOB
Well let's sit, Momma. Let's sit near the house here where there's some shade.

[*They walk closer to 121.*]

VERA
I wonder how cool this house is in the summer?

JACOB
It doesn't seem to get too hot inside. I'm going inside later to do some plaster work on the walls. It has indoor plumbing.

VERA
There are only a few houses on the reservation that have indoor plumbing.

JACOB
Yeah. It would be nice not having to haul water.

VERA
What about electricity?

JACOB
Now, Momma, you know every single one of these white houses have indoor plumbing, electricity, and some have those new, what are they called, televisions things.

VERA
Must be nice.

JACOB
Are you wishing, my little momma?

> [*She makes a place for them on the ground to sit. She removes sandwiches wrapped in cheese cloth.*]

Man, that smells good.

VERA
Some of that deer roast from last night. My mom told me to go ahead and slice it for sandwiches. There are some tomatoes and some cucumber chips. I put ketchup on yours.

JACOB
Boy, you feed me good, Momma.

VERA
I know, *aye!* Now eat.

[*They look at each other and share a gentle kiss.*]

JACOB
You know what? I'm glad you picked me from the rest of the herd.

VERA
Settle down, Jacob.

121
Hhh . . . ow . . . Swee . . .

VERA
Did you hear that?

JACOB
Yes. I think it's the meadowlarks and the sparrows that are nesting in the bushes over there, around the side of the house.

VERA
It didn't sound like any birds I've heard before.

JACOB
Well, it couldn't have been anything else but birds. We are the only ones here. Old Man Peterson is in town. Her highness is in town at the bank. I'm supposed to be pull weeds, check the fencing on the lot, and take a look at the backyard for a garden. Oh. Come here, my beautiful wife. I have something to show you.

[*He stands.*]

VERA
What? What is it, Jacob?

JACOB
This morning, after pulling weeds around the house and porch, I started to look in the backyard for a site to start a garden. Peterson wants me to spade and break up the ground for a small plot garden. I was walking around when I found this.

[*He leads her to an area close to* 121. 121 *is watching.*]

See?

VERA
What is it?

JACOB
Remember my grandpa Yellow Robe?

VERA
Your mom's father.

JACOB
Yeah. That's the one. He told me about these a long time ago. He took me to the Little Frog Creek area and while we were hunting we discovered this old campsite.

VERA
Really? Our people?

JACOB
Yes. Long before there was an agency, rations, enrollment. When a family made a home out of the simplest of things. There were three of these teepee rings on the side of the hill near the creek. They had this small pit lined with rocks. There were other rocks to the side of the pit. This is how they cooked back then. They would put hot stones into the buffalo's belly when they made soup. Look.

[*He points to a half circle of rocks and a small pit.*]

VERA
What is this? Are you saying this is an Indian family's home?

JACOB
A long time ago, maybe. The people who bought this land didn't know what these are. They just assumed it was a path of rocks. See these rocks here. The one in a half circle? This is a teepee ring. The other half of it, the rocks there, they have been picked and were probably used as part of the foundation for the house.

VERA
Is that a bad thing, Jacob?

JACOB
I don't think so. They didn't know. Remember, they came out here to our homes and changed everything to suit their lives. It didn't matter what they did. They changed everything to fit them. Our homes became their homes.

VERA
Oh yes. I remember now. I've heard stories about the teepee rings but I've never seen them.

JACOB
You weren't supposed to see them or even know about them. Most of the older ones out in the country are plowed over, or picked up and discarded to make way for the farmers and their wheat fields. They are the marks of old-time Indian homes. They are all gone now. Just like we are supposed to be—never mind what I said, Vera.

VERA
You're telling the truth. Why should I mind when my husband tells the truth? You know what, Jacob? I wonder if that means that this house is part Indian.

JACOB
Better not tell those agency people or they'll force it to come in, sign papers, and they'll assign it a new name and an enrollment number. The last thing will be a priest to convert it.

VERA
Hello, cousin house.

121
Hi . . . hi . . . hel-lo. . . .

VERA
My husband, are you sure everything is all right with this house?

JACOB
Why? What happened? What did you hear?

VERA
I'm going back to work Jacob. Where I won't hear things that aren't real.

[*She begins to gather their lunch.*]

JACOB
Vera, what did you hear? I didn't really hear anything. Honest.

VERA
You didn't hear that, that voice?

JACOB
Just the beating of your heart, *aye!* No, what voice?

VERA
Jacob. It sounded, sounded like a, a female.

JACOB
What did it say?

VERA
I couldn't make it out. It was such a soft whisper. It sounded like, like someone saying "hi," or "hello"?

JACOB
That isn't so bad. No, come on Vera. If it were something bad, like if someone telling us to "get out," or "go away." It would be bad. This is a greeting.

VERA
When you come home, before you enter our home, you take care of yourself. Do you promise.

JACOB
I will. I always do. I'll take care of this, Vera. If we were to ever get this house, or a house like it. I promise you I'll take steps to make sure it is safe for you, me, our families. I promise.

VERA
Oh. I will hold you to your own words, my husband.

JACOB
I want you to think of his. One day, since things have changed. If a family has to have a fine house like this to be considered by other as a "respectful" family. I'll make sure we have it.

VERA
I don't need this, Jacob. I just need you. And one of those new washing machines, *aye!* Or a pony! *Aye!*

Blackout. End of Act One.

Act Two

SCENE ONE

CHRISTEN *sits in a metal folding chair. There is a full-size mattress on a box spring in their area. It has faded sheets and a thin, worn comforter on it. There are a few pillows, but they are old and stained. There is an ashtray at the side of* CHRISTEN's *chair.* SAM *is standing holding a cup of coffee.*

CHRISTEN
Sam, Daddy, don't get mad at me. I've heard something. I heard this off and on for over a year now. I just can't stand to hear these kinds of stories, but everyone in town is pointing at me and you can hear them whisper to each other. It makes me sick.

SAM
Stories about us? What are they saying?

CHRISTEN
Not about me, or you and me, but mostly about you.

SAM
Oh. Those stories? The ones from the past, huh?

CHRISTEN
Are they true?

SAM
No, but do you believe them? I mean, there will always be stories about me, even you and the little one. Can't run every time we hear one of these stories. No matter who tells it, or how believable they make it sound. It comes down to just us being a family and sticking together.

CHRISTEN
I know it's about us being a family, but yesterday at my mother's, she had her Indian friend stop by, and this Indian friend started questioning me about who I was married to and whatnot. Then she just sat there and told me this really bad story about you. Something that happened a long time ago?

SAM
Do you believe her?

CHRISTEN
No. I can't. She made me feel so bad. I didn't get mad and yell at her. I knew it was a lie. Sam, I can't believe all those stories. After all you've done for me and Mary, our family.

SAM
I was sixteen and raised a lot of hell when I was young. People will always say some shit about people they don't like.

CHRISTEN
I can never understand how somebody could say such mean and vicious things about people they don't even know.

SAM
You don't? I do. Jealousy! They are just jealous. They see an Indin married to a pretty white woman and they think I'm acting too high and mighty. So they make up some real vicious stories about me. No good racists . . . ah!

CHRISTEN
You are right, Poppa. There are some white people who are telling me the same stories. Saying the same things.

SAM
Indian, white, just plain jealous bad people. They don't want to see an Indin with a white girl. Your mom wasn't crazy when you told her that you were

going to marry me. They don't get the idea that we are in love. That's all it is, baby girl. Come here.

[CHRISTEN *does.*]

Here, my baby girl. Here is some sweet love for your poppa. Don't worry about what people say about me. You and I know the truth and that's all that matters.

CHRISTEN
I love you, Poppa.

SAM
I know you do. I love you too.

CHRISTEN
And Mary?

SAM
Yeah? What about her?

CHRISTEN
You love her too? Just like your own daughter?

SAM
Even more.

[*They kiss, and he begins to laugh.*]

Lights fade. Blackout. End of scene.

SCENE TWO

Lights up in area with 121 *and* LEROY. 121 *is sitting on the ground holding her side. Leroy is sitting and facing her.*

121
This pain. I've never felt anything like it before.

LEROY
It'll pass. It won't be long now. Is there anything else that is bothering you?

121
I feel strange. I feel like there are things inside of me, all through me, but I can't describe these feelings.

LEROY
Can you hold on?

121
Yes, but they are alive. They are all coming in a rush.

LEROY
It won't be long. Just stay with me if you can.

121
Some of these, these things, they are rushing through me. Then just in a brief moment, like a breath, one stays in place just long enough for me to—to see it, or feel it. Before I can really see it, or recognize it, it's gone. It seems so odd. Am I dying?

LEROY
You better not be. I don't feel what I'm doing is going to make it worse for you. It will get better. I promise you.

121
What is causing this? Why now? I felt I was asleep. I was sleeping for so long, and now I'm awake. Am I? I'm awake and I don't know why?

LEROY
After many years, some folks, maybe a certain few, can't recall the simplest of things. I think you are feeling, or hearing, all those things from the past that most people would never remember or would try to forget.

121
Did you have anything to do with this?

LEROY
No—yes, I guess in some ways. A little bit, but not all of it.

121
What part?

LEROY
I have nothing to do with the things that are inside of you. I didn't make those.

121
But?

LEROY
In some ways, what I've been doing is making things inside of you move, to come out.

121
Are you saying you gave me something?

LEROY
Like meds, or something?

121
Meds?

LEROY
Uh, no. I didn't think it would turn out this way.

121
What would turn out, what way?

LEROY
Well, first of all, I didn't think I could talk with you.

121
Here I am.

LEROY
I know, but I didn't think it would be, you know, like this. In this way.

121
What "way" did you expect?

LEROY
Nothing. I wasn't expecting anything because it's been so long. There hasn't been anybody here in a long time. My folks told me about the other people . . .

121
I see people every day. I saw people yesterday and earlier today.

LEROY
You're sure they're people?

121
Yes. Just like seeing you this morning. I wanted to come out to talk with you, but something, or someone, wouldn't allow me to leave, or be near you.

LEROY
You want to be near me?

121
Yes. Isn't that what every person wants? To be near somebody? To share something with somebody? "Especially if they love them," I heard that, *aye*.

LEROY
Uh, do you remember some of these people you've seen?

121
Not all of them, but a few of them.

LEROY
Do you remember their names?

121
I don't know. I can barely remember what they looked like. There seem to be so many of them.

LEROY
And this all happened just today?

121
Well, not just today. I can recall a moment. I could see some bodies, or see a face. I can hear a whisper of a voice, or voices. I look to see if I could find the voice, or even the smells of these people, but I can't find them. I found myself looking for a person, something. I didn't find anything. It's like a shadow. Not just one, but sometimes it was like having several of them appear in a room, and when I walk over to them they are gone. They would seem to appear without light. Isn't that odd?

LEROY
Like a ghost?

121
What?

LEROY
Do you know what ghosts are, 121?

121
Yes. No. Ghosts are—what are those?

LEROY
There are stories different people tell of these spirits that linger after someone has died. Sometimes when a person died a hard or bad death, their spirit lingers in that space where they passed.

121
Is that one of the beliefs of your people?

LEROY
Yeah, but not all of my family, or relatives, but a few of us believe.

121
I've only known Christians. I don't think they believe in those things. I don't.

LEROY
Are you Christian, too?

121
I—I don't know.

LEROY
Do you believe in ghosts, or spirits?

121
I just said—I don't know—now—I mean—

LEROY
We'll find out before the day is out, so don't worry.

121
What's causing these pains? I've never had these pains before, not until today. They are sharp, but they don't last long. Not long, but short and sharp.

LEROY
Couldn't really say what they are. I remember when I was a kid. I was playing in a field and fell down on some cactus. I had all these needles in my hand and fingers. I picked every needle out of my fingers and hand. It wasn't so bad, but I can almost remember each that I pulled out of my flesh.

121
Did you cry?

LEROY
At first, yeah, because I was scared. I was just a kid.

121
Well, I'm certainly no child.

LEROY
Younger than a rock or a tree, and to some, just as important?

121
What? What did you say?

LEROY
It was something I heard. Not long ago. It just came to me.

121
I asked this before, Leroy.

LEROY
Yes. That's my name.

121
I've asked this question before, Leroy. You are an American Indian, but what am I?

LEROY
I don't know. You should know that yourself. I mean. You aren't really from here, but you've become a part of this world. I imagine a lot of people are responsible for you being here.

121
I just didn't spring out of nowhere, right? I was—I was born.

LEROY
Yeah—no—I mean. It isn't an easy question that I can answer right now.

121
But you know, Leroy?

LEROY
I sort of know. Our folks keep track of everybody who is a member of our family, or who we are related to. We don't write it down, we just recall.

121
Is it accurate? I mean, is it always right?

LEROY
For us it is. A lot of it isn't written, but you can find two or three people who can follow up a story and add more details to it.

121
Do you know any stories about me? Am I part American Indian? I'm not "white."

LEROY
Well, "white" isn't a culture, but a color. I know you've looked different in color at different times.

121
What? What do you mean?

LEROY
You aren't "white," but I don't think you are American Indian or Indin. You could be a lot of things, far beyond any of our labels.

121
When you were a boy and pulled the needles of the cactus from your hand and fingers?

LEROY
Yes?

121
You said you cried, did you stop? Why?

LEROY
I faced my fear, and then I got used to the pain.

121
Leroy?

LEROY
Yes.

121
Will I cry?

Lights fade. Blackout. End of scene.

SCENE THREE

Lights up on another part of the stage. We see a Native Man, JACOB EAGLES, *and his wife,* VERA EAGLES, *entering the lit area. They are carrying leather*

1940s suitcases and some Pendleton and US Army blankets. VERA *holds a wooden box filled with some household items.* VERA *sets the wooden box on the floor.*

JACOB
Here we are, Momma. I didn't bring you a string of ponies when we got married, but I bought the fort for you.

VERA
Oh, stink, Jacob. It's still nice.

JACOB
We have a yearlong lease. I called the Petersons and the old man signed it this morning.

VERA
Veronica said yes? And can we really afford the rent?

JACOB
I have an option to buy it. So, after the year is up, we can decide if this is where we want to be.

VERA
This is so nice.

[*She walks around the house.*]

Imagine what it will be like when we have our families in here.

JACOB
Yeah, it'll be big enough, just about right. In fact, they should be showing up tomorrow to take a look. We should go out and get some makings for a big pot of soup. Maybe even throw in a roast.

VERA
I can't believe Greg Peterson would rent it to us.

JACOB
Well, I've worked for that family for the last ten years. I've been everything from a plumber, carpenter, electrician, painter, to a referee for his family. I

think he gave up on the idea of saving it for his family. Veronica showed no interest in it. When he was talking about advertising it, I spoke up and made him an offer.

121
Hello, Vera.

VERA
What was that? Jacob? Did you hear it?

JACOB
It could be the house settling. It's an old house. I was working upstairs last summer and we've done a lot of painting. The foundation isn't like one of those FHA houses. It has a foundation of stone.

VERA
Are we going to hear those sounds all the time?

JACOB
Maybe. The house has to be over seventy years old.

VERA
We've lived in some worse places—Oh! I don't mean it like that, Jacob.

JACOB
Yeah. I know you didn't. It is a lot better than living with your cousins. I was getting used to the idea of having my suitcase as a dresser bureau and a bed sheet for a wall.

VERA
I can't believe it's so quiet. I'm so used to hearing the sounds of all our nieces and nephews.

JACOB
We'll actually be alone. No more waiting for the bathroom, or waiting to take a shower. We can listen to the radio when we want to, and as late as we want to. I can put another radio in our bedroom, if you want me to, or I can just sing to you.

VERA
The families didn't bother me that bad, Jacob. I'm going to sort of miss them. They are my family too.

JACOB
I didn't mean it that way, baby.

121
Ind-family . . .

JACOB
Whoa. I've never heard anything like that before.

VERA
What is it, Jacob?

JACOB
Pipes? I don't know. Maybe we should smudge before we—

[*There is a knock. The sound of the door opening.*]

Hello.

[VERONICA PETERSON *enters. She is the daughter of the landlord,* GREG PETERSON. *Behind her is the County Deputy Sheriff,* DOUG JENSEN.]

VERONICA
Hello? Chief? Is that you, Jacob?

DOUG
Official business, Jacob.

[*They enter the space.* VERONICA *holds an official court envelope.*]

JACOB
Come in, come in. We just got here ourselves. We were just getting unpacked.

VERONICA
Maybe we'll save you the effort.

DOUG
Please, Veronica.

JACOB
What's going on, Miss Peterson?

VERA
Jacob? What's going on?

VERONICA
This doesn't concern your wife, Jacob. There's only you two in here, right?

DOUG
Let me . . . I don't know how to tell you this, Jacob.

JACOB
What? What is it?

VERONICA
I want you folks out of my house by five o'clock today.

VERA
What? We have a lease.

DOUG
It turns out Greg doesn't have the authority to have signed the lease with Jacob. Veronica, here, has power of attorney over her dad's properties and she went to court and had the court dissolve the lease.

JACOB
Dissolved? They broke our lease? How is that possible? We have a copy of it too, and it's signed and witnessed. This isn't right, Doug. You know that.

VERONICA
But not by me—the rightful owner of the house and property. If it were signed by me, I wouldn't be here right now. I have the final say as to who

is going to be living in my house and on my land. If I had signed the lease, I would be locked up and medicated. It's bad business to rent to you people. My own father told me that.

JACOB
You watched me work on this house all summer long. You sat in your car and watched me work in the yard all day long without saying word. You've never mentioned that you owned it.

VERONICA
Look, Jacob, this isn't hard to understand. I own the house. You weren't working for my dad, you work for me. Know your place. I never mentioned I would rent or lease it to you. You shouldn't take it so hard, Jacob. You Indians get free medicine and houses. I would never rent to a colored, so why would I rent to you people?

JACOB
Your dad gave me a lease with the option to buy this house.

VERONICA
Well, my dad believes in flying saucers and little green men. He actually believes a black man will be president one day.

DOUG
Veronica, let me handle this! If you want to hire an attorney and take this to court, you can, Jacob. You'll have to go to our court system, but I'm going to have to ask you and your wife to remove yourselves and your things from this house today.

VERONICA
Five o'clock today. No later. You folks do own some type of timepiece?

VERA
This isn't right, Doug. Can he really do this?

DOUG
I'm sorry, Vera, but she is the legal owner of the house and property.

JACOB
Why didn't your father tell me this before I signed?

VERONICA
My father has problems. That's the reason why I have the power of attorney for him. What part of "power of attorney" don't you understand, Jacob? It's the way we white people take care of our old people. If you Indians were civilized, you'd be doing the same thing.

JACOB
Veronica, this isn't right. I have a lease, a contract.

VERONICA
And I have an eviction notice from the proper courts that says you and wife have to get out of here. Look, if you and your, your squaw don't vacate my house by the end of the day you'll both be locked up—

[JACOB *moves on* VERONICA. DOUG *stops him.*]

JACOB
Don't you disgrace my—

DOUG
Hold it! Don't you dare Jacob!

VERA
Jacob! Jacob! Don't let her bother you. We'll—we'll hire an attorney and follow this through their court.

VERONICA
You can be taught, but remember, it won't be in federal court. You won't have the advantage—

DOUG
Veronica, if you're done, go!

JACOB
What about the rent money and deposit we paid? Your father took that. I want that back.

VERONICA
Sure. Show me the receipt, and I'll send you a check for it. I'll hold onto

the deposit and have a look at the place after you leave. Just in case I have to have it cleaned, again. Glad we came when we did, otherwise we'd have a whole pack of you to kick out. Like damn bugs. I'll have to have this house fumigated.

[*She exits.*]

VERA
Doug, how can this be? How can she do this?

DOUG
I'm sorry, Vera, but she's the legal owner. I don't think you can get the Tribe to help you out on this one. If this were on the reservation I'm sure it wouldn't be—

VERA
That's a lie. Even on the reservation, she would still have the power to do this and no one would stop her. They could arrest us, but she would always be free.

JACOB
Be honest with me, Doug. Do we have a chance if we go to the county court?

DOUG
I don't know. It would depend on whose court you have to go to. Jensen doesn't like coloreds or Indians. Denholt doesn't like anybody. You might lose your rent money and deposit. I don't know what attorney would represent you. Most of the attorneys around here are like Veronica. They don't like Indians.

VERA
We just got here, Doug. We haven't had a chance to open or take anything out.

DOUG
I'm sorry, Jacob, Vera. I really am.

JACOB
Are you going to enforce the notice?

DOUG
I'll have too.

JACOB
That means we have—

DOUG
A little over two hours to get all your belongings out of the house.

JACOB
All of it? I had my brothers and cousins help me move this furniture into the house. I don't know if I can call them in time to help me move it out.

DOUG
You just have to get it out of the house, Jacob.

VERA
And if we don't, you'll arrest us?

DOUG
Yes.

JACOB
They used to say we had to leave the reservation to make a better life. How better is this life?

DOUG
I'll be outside, folks.

VERA
Well, I can walk down to the store and call your brothers and mine—

JACOB
Goddamn it!

VERA
Jacob! What's wrong? Don't get mad, not now. I need you to keep your head so we can get this done.

JACOB
I know, Vera, but this isn't right. It isn't right! I fought in a war, for whose freedom?! Not ours!

VERA
Jacob. Please. Calm down. We don't want war right now.

[*She holds him.*]

I know. It wasn't right when we were kids, and it isn't right now.

JACOB
What I should do is—is . . .

VERA
No. We will just get our things out of this house. I'll call my family and your family. We will move our things out and check to see if we have to sweep, mop, and clean. We can take our belongings and store them at different places, and tomorrow we'll try to find an attorney and . . .

JACOB
Go to *their* court looking for justice and getting nothing.

VERA
You don't know that, Jacob. It's not like our grandparents' times. They could never do the things we can do today.

JACOB
It ends the same way. Except the land is taken a second time, our home was never started, and there are no troops to push us, just a sheriff with a piece of paper.

VERA
Where's your sweet grass?

JACOB
What?

VERA
Offer a prayer for us, Jacob? Please?

JACOB
I don't know if I can. My heart doesn't feel right—

VERA
I will, if you want me to, but it needs to be done. We have and always will have our heart.

JACOB
For us?

VERA
For all of us. Go from room to room and offer something good for all of us. I'll start taking our things outside and go and call our folks.

JACOB
You really want me?

VERA
Now, especially now.

JACOB
All right.

[*She begins to pick some items off the floor watching* JACOB *as he removes a shell and a braid of sweet grass from a cedar box. She starts to exit.*]

I can't do it. I can't do it right now because the anger is too strong. I'm sorry, but I promise you that one day, I will return. I'll finish this. I promise you that.

Lights fade. Light up in MARY's *room. It is a different location onstage. Her room from Act One. She sits on the floor playing with some toys. She hears a noise of the house.*

MARY
Hello.

[121 *stands to the side with one arm raised, suggesting a door.* 121 *doesn't respond.*]

Kona? Who is it? Is that you, my *Kona*?

[121 *lifts a piece of clothing.*]

You shouldn't be here. I wish I wasn't here. My daddy wants to play his favorite game again. I don't want to do it. I wish my mom was here. I wish I could tell her.

[121 *drops the clothing.*]

I wish someone will help me. I don't want to play.

[*Sounds of somebody walking up the stairs.* MARY *is terrified and tries to hide.* SAM *enters. He is nearly naked.* 121 *moves as if the door is closing.*]

SAM
Mary? Mary? Where are you? Sweet baby girl.

[121 *is terrified being a witness.*]

Come on. Your ma's at work. Get out here. Mary! It's time to play our game of injured animal and the little princess. I know you like it.

[MARY *appears from her hiding place.*]

MARY
Please, no, Dad. I don't want to.

SAM
No, what? Don't be this way, little sweetie. Come on. You don't want to upset your dad?

MARY
No. I don't want to upset you, Dad, but I don't want to play this game.

SAM
Come on, yes you do, play with your daddy, Mary. Be a good baby girl. See. I'm an animal who is wounded. . . .

[MARY *runs to* 121 *and struggles to open the door.*]

Now what the hell are you doing?

[*He grabs her and tosses her to the other side of the room.*]

You're getting the furry happy animal angry! The mean evil animal is coming out. Now come over and get on the bed.

[*He jumps on the bed.*]

Come on. Come over here and help the wounded animal. Only you know how to help the wounded animal. You do this a lot better than your mother. Your mother doesn't know how to do this. You are a lot better than your mom.

MARY
I don't want to do this. I don't like this game.

SAM
Yeah. I wouldn't be asking you to do this if your mother knew how to do it. Come on over. I'm not mad. I haven't told anybody. It's our secret.

MARY
It hurts. Every time we do this, it hurts.

SAM
I'll be gentle. I promise. Now come over here.

[MARY *slowly approaches the bed.*]

Come on, sweetie. There you go, daddy's sweetheart.

[*She bolts for* 121 *and starts to pull on the door.* SAM *laughs.*]

Little bitch! I locked it.

[MARY *begins to cry. 121 watches* MARY *and suddenly moves her arm, like the door opening. We hear* CHRISTEN *calling.*]

CHRISTEN

[*Calling.*]

I'm back, and I brought Nana with me.

MARY
Grandma!

[121 *tries to yell along with* MARY.]

MARY AND 121
Help me/her! Help me/her! Daddy's/he is hurting us! Help!

[MARY *exits.* SAM *is terrified.*]

CHRISTEN
Oh my god!

MARY

[*Offstage.*]

He hurts me, Grandma! Daddy is trying to hurt me! Momma! Help me.

SAM
Uh—uh—I didn't do anything, Christen. It wasn't my fault. Listen to me. Let me explain.

[SAM *runs to* 121, *but* 121 *moves the arm like a door shutting.* SAM *tries desperately to get out but can't.* 121 *glares at him.*]

She is telling a lie! I would never . . . she's a liar!

[121 *picks up a toy and throws it at* SAM. *He is terrified and is silent.*]

Blackout. End of scene.

SCENE FOUR

Lights up in the area of LEROY *and* 121. LEROY *is standing and* 121 *sits.*

121
Remember how I told you I could hear voices and sometimes see the faces of people?

LEROY
Yes.

121
There are some who I think are very bad. I think I do not ever want to hear them or even try to remember what they look like. I don't even want to feel them. The worst thing is that they've touched me. They've touched me and no matter how hard I try to rid myself of them, they come back a little stronger. There are some of these voices that are so soft and nice. So gentle. When I try to remember them and how they look, I find it difficult to remember them. Isn't that funny? Why is that, Leroy?

LEROY
What? Living with memories?

121
Or am I being with my memories? Why is it that I can almost touch my memories, but not know them?

LEROY
That happens a lot. It isn't anything new. Don't worry.

121
You don't know either, huh? Oh!

[*A sharp pain.*]

LEROY
Are you okay?

121
I don't know. I just felt a, a memory. Something happened a long time ago. I think. It comes back to me. The images and sounds. I can see a picture and it comes to life. This one really causes a lot of pain.

LEROY
Is it from a long time ago?

121
I don't know. It seems so odd. I guess it isn't so different from what's happening now, is it? I see this image, or picture, of a little girl. I can almost remember her name. She looks so frightened. So afraid of—I don't know, but there is a real fear in her eyes.

LEROY
From how long ago?

121
I don't know. I don't know if it happened a few days ago or so long ago. I remember watching her. She is seeking someone to help her. She's crying out, but I don't remember what her words are. I think no one hears her words. No one is coming.

LEROY
Why was she afraid?

121
There's someone else with her. She's afraid of this person. I can't see the other person, but only the little girl. This is one of those things I want to forget.

LEROY
Do you feel responsible for what is happening?

121
Responsible?

LEROY
There being a little girl in such fear and not being able to do something to help her?

121
I think—I think I did—do. Leroy? But how could I be responsible?

LEROY
Yes, you've become part of a lie.

121
I don't want to. I'm—I'm just there. I don't even know why I'm there. I'm just standing and see the picture. I might have done something if I could find, or have, a reason.

LEROY
So why does this picture return to you?

121
I don't have a reason, but, but I think I did something.

LEROY
Do you remember?

121
Are you being sarcastic?

LEROY
No. I'm just surprised.

121
I did something.

LEROY
What did you do?

121
I—I—I created an opening.

LEROY
What do you mean?

121
I made it possible for her to leave that picture. I gave her an opening and closed it right after she entered it, so no one could follow her.

LEROY
And the man, or thing, that was scaring her?

121
I made sure no one followed her. She got out. Have you ever done anything like that, Leroy?

LEROY
Yes. Sometimes I have. It doesn't work all the time, but I have managed to help a few get out by making an opening.

121
It would be a good thing if we could do that for all people.

LEROY
They are there, but some folks don't know what they are looking at and when to enter it, or leave.

Light fade. Blackout. End of scene.

SCENE FIVE

The light comes up in the area of NEIL *and* CALVIN. CALVIN *is eating a sandwich.* NEIL *is wearing some welding glasses and has on a heavy coat. He is eating a sandwich and drinking a soda.*

NEIL
I shouldn't have said a word about the food. Now it'll be another hour before you get back to work.

CALVIN
What's that thing in your hand?

NEIL
I need to keep up the energy levels. I've been putting in a hard day.

[CALVIN *gets up and crosses the stage and stops.*]

What?

CALVIN
Hey, that old guy is still out there.

NEIL
What's he doing?

CALVIN
Looks like he's talking to somebody.

NEIL
Who is it?

CALVIN
The old Indin guy.

NEIL
No numb nuts. Who is he talking to?

CALVIN
Whoa, this is weird, but there isn't anybody there.

NEIL
What?

CALVIN
Yeah. He's talking away, and there is no one there.

NEIL
Damn. What kind of Indin are you? He's probably praying.

CALVIN
Praying?

NEIL
"Our lord, who farts in heaven." Yeah, praying. He was smoking the place up earlier this morning. Remember?

CALVIN
Yeah, but he's making some weird hand motions.

NEIL
Maybe he's listening to music and making some fancy rez moves. Like those old colored singing groups, Charlie Pride.

CALVIN
I know I know this guy, but I can't think of his name.

NEIL
Hurry up and finish your grub. I'll go downstairs and knock this out. I want to go out to the casino tonight. I think it's the fish buffet. I really like the way they make those deep-fried frog legs with the deep-fried cheese.

CALVIN
If they could deep fry Spam, you'd eat that, too.

NEIL
Yeah. Good eats.

CALVIN
Hey, Neil?

NEIL
What?

CALVIN
How much do I get for doing this work for you?

NEIL
Don't know. Not off the top of my head. Say, ten bucks an hour, meals—

CALVIN
What meals? Food bank sandwiches you stole, or stashed?

NEIL
All right, twelve bucks an hour.

CALVIN
And the things you've taken out of the house. The stain glass, copper pipes, those old steam heaters.

NEIL
They're all mine.

CALVIN
Yeah, but I was the one who helped you take them out and loaded them for you. I should get a cut out of that scrap materials.

NEIL
I can't say, because I don't know what I'll get for it.

121
Put . . . place it . . .

NEIL
What the hell is making that noise?

121
. . . it back—

CALVIN
See! Did you hear it?

NEIL
We're just tired. It could be a lot of things. Since we took some of the bones out of the walls, it could be just a shifting.

CALVIN
Is this place going to come down on us?

NEIL
No. I braced it with some scrap beams. Are you finished?

CALVIN
Yeah, "It was real goot cuzin"! Too bad we couldn't get some hot sandwiches for a change.

NEIL
After I say we're done, you can eat all the Big Macs and Whoppers you want, but we have to finish this rodeo. Where's the tank and the torch?

CALVIN
I put them downstairs where you wanted them.

[NEIL *gets up and exits the area.*]

NEIL
Clean up here and come downstairs. There are more pipes and tubes I want to take out tonight.

CALVIN
Scared somebody might see you do it in the daylight?

NEIL
No. Hurry up.

[*He exits.* CALVIN *sits and continues to eat.*]

CALVIN
Where does he get this food at? I know it wasn't the food bank. He probably was dumpster diving at the gas station.

121
Oww!

[NEIL *calling.*]

NEIL
Stop playing around up there. If you're finished, get down here and give me a hand.

CALVIN
Wasn't me! What are you doing now?

NEIL

> [*Calling.*]

Trying to cut this pipe. Hey, I could use more light down here. Go to my truck and get that lantern.

CALVIN
Where's it at? In the bed?

NEIL

> [*Calling.*]

Yeah. Bring my smokes while you are at it.

> [CALVIN *gets up and begins to cross. He comes to a halt.*]

CALVIN
What the hell . . .

> [*He tries again but is halted.*]

This is some weird—

NEIL

> [*Calling.*]

Hurry up!

CALVIN
I'm trying.

NEIL

> [*Calling.*]

What are you talking about? Stop playing around!

CALVIN
I'm not. I, I, I can't get out of this house.

NEIL

[*Calling.*]

You want me to come up and show you how to open the door?

CALVIN
No, but I can't get out. The door won't open.

NEIL

[*Calling.*]

It could be jammed. Force it, and we'll duct tape it later when we leave.

CALVIN
Okay!

[*He struggles, trying to get out of the area but can't.*]

Damn!

[*He can't get out.*]

Hey!

NEIL

[*Calling.*]

I'm busy!

CALVIN
This is really weird, man.

NEIL

    [*Calling.*]

Oh for goddamn sakes! What is your problem?!

CALVIN
I can't get out.

NEIL

    [*Calling.*]

I'll finish cutting this pipe, and I'll come up!

CALVIN
Maybe that old guy can help. Hey!

    [*He is calling to* LEROY *who doesn't respond.*]

Hey! Hey, brother!

    [*No response.*]

Hey, man! Heya', heya'—hey, old Indin guy!

    [*No response.*]

Help me out with this door!

    [*No response.*]

Look this way!

    [*No response.*]

Who is he talking to? Hey!

    [*No response.*]

Old Indin guy—look this way! Hey!

[*No response.*]

Hey, I'm trapped in here with a crazy half-breed with a blow torch going after some—

[*No response.*]

Neil! Be careful so you don't—

[*There is a loud explosion.* CALVIN *freezes. He doesn't move.*]

Lights fade. Blackout. End of scene.

SCENE SIX

Lights up in the area of LEROY *and* 121. 121 *is on the ground having a convulsion of pain.* LEROY *watches and is smudging* 121.

LEROY
121, hey there, 121?

[*No response.*]

121, can you hear me?

[*No response.*]

121, if you can, tell me what is wrong?

121
Inside of me. It is inside of me!

LEROY
Pain, again?

121
A lot of pain! I think, I think . . . Leroy, I'm broken. . . .

LEROY
Can you move?

121
I'll try.

[121 *slowly moves.*]

LEROY
Can you move?

121
I don't know what it is, but something is holding me. Holding me to the ground.

LEROY
Take your time.

121
Oww! It hurts! This pain . . .

LEROY
Can you stand? Please, try to stand.

121
I don't know. I'm scared. What if I can't?

[121 *slowly stands.*]

I, I can breathe, but it feels like I'm empty inside of me and all around my body is so heavy.

LEROY
That's a good sign.

121
Why? Because I'm . . . No! No! Leroy. I'm not dead, am I? I can't be! I can . . .

LEROY
No, by no means are you dead, or even near death.

121
You're right. It feels so different. Not like before. What's happened to me?

LEROY
Don't be afraid.

121
What's happening to me, Leroy?

LEROY
I think you're ready.

121
Ready for what?

LEROY
Well, slowly walk towards me.

121
Why, what'll happen?

LEROY
We'll see when you walk to me.

121
You won't run away?

LEROY
If I run, you could catch me, at least this time.

[121 *slowly walks toward* LEROY *and then comes to a slow halt.*]

121
I can't. It's the same as before.

LEROY
Don't stop. Keep moving.

121
I don't think I can. It feels like something is grabbing on to me. Holding me.

LEROY
Just keep moving.

121
It reminds me of your story. It's like I have all these little needles in me and they are slowly coming out, one by one.

LEROY
Yeah, but keep moving.

[LEROY *steps back.*]

121
Where are you going? You said you wouldn't leave!

LEROY
Just keep moving. Come to me, 121.

[*Holds out his hand and* 121 *reaches for his hand.*]

121
I can reach you. I can—

[121 *grabs* LEROY's *hand.* 121 *becomes aware of self.* 121 *is aged, but not ancient.*]

121
I made it.

LEROY
You did it.

121
I'm here, but where was—

[121 *looks back at an image on a screen of a house that is nearly gone. It is fire damaged, with broken windows, the yard is littered, and a broken fence surrounds it. It was a large house, but a fire from the past has burned its roof and the second floor and part of the first floor. Some of the black wood frame stands.*]

121
That's—that was me? I'm that thing?

LEROY
Yes, you were.

121
What happened to me?

LEROY
It was a long time ago, about five years ago.

121
Then I am dead. You lied to me!

LEROY
No. That's dead, you are alive.

121
What am I?

LEROY
You are, or were, 121 East Hampshire. I don't know what to call you now. A spirit?

121
A ghost?

LEROY
No. A ghost means you died. You are a spirit that was made there. Just like all life. We need a place to start.

121
I wasn't alone, was I? I had—I had families, people, with—within me? Where are they?

LEROY
They are gone. Some of them left this area. Some of them passed on. Some are waiting to pass on.

> [LEROY *points behind* 121 *and a slow parade of some of the people walk by. They don't acknowledge or see* 121 *and* LEROY. CALVIN *and* NEIL *are the first to leave, followed by* CHRISTEN, *and finally,* MARY.]

121
I know her. That little one.

LEROY
Yes, but they don't know you, not now.

121
I—I will miss them.

LEROY
Let them start their own journey. You've held onto them for a long time. You've done good by them.

121
Me? What do I do now?

LEROY
Go. Go wherever you want to. There is nothing to hold you now.

121
I'm—I'm alive?

LEROY
You were always alive. People, couples, families, all of them made you come to life. You were both good and bad to some, but you didn't really have a say in it.

121
The little girl. I feel so bad for what happened to her. It wasn't my fault. Is that why I couldn't leave?

LEROY
No. You supported whatever life came to you. You can't be held responsible for what others brought to you. It's just that, well, when people left, they left something of themselves here and what they left was never released. This area has always had this heavy feeling when I walked passed you. The weight you were bearing was held here, it held you too.

121
A reason?

LEROY
My grandson told me when he was in his science class he learned that life is made up of atoms. You never know what kind of life they'll make or bring. You can only watch and see what kind of life is made. You were allowed to watch all the atoms, but you couldn't have a hand in how the atoms would create a life.

121
What do I do next, Leroy? Where will I go?

LEROY
Don't be afraid. You have freedom now. Never be afraid of freedom because we were all given that.

[*Blackout. End of play.*]

Frog's Dance

Characters

FROG JUMPS THE GROUND, a man in his late forties
ELMO BLAINE, a teenager
ELAINE JUMPS THE GROUND, a spirit, in her early thirties
NINA, a woman in her early twenties, wife to Frog
TYLER GRANT, a man in his late forties
EMERSON, a teenager
DENISE, a teenager
NELLIE, a teenager
DANCER and WARCRAFT DANCERS, Frog's and Elmo's tormentors
ERVIN BIRD, a man in his late seventies
MINA FLYNN, a woman in her late sixties
MC ANNOUNCER, in his mid-fifties
Various DANCERS of various styles

PROLOGUE

FROG *is onstage. He is dancing and enjoying himself. In the upstage area we see two unrecognizable Tribal* DANCERS. *The two* DANCERS *slowly move downstage and join* FROG. *One of the* DANCERS *takes a black cloth and lays it on the side of* FROG's *face.* FROG *winces in pain. The second* DANCER *takes another black cloth and lays it on* FROG's *leg. This causes* FROG *to lose the use of his leg. The two* DANCERS *exit.* FROG *struggles to dance. He stumbles and begins to fall.*

FROG
Nina! I'm falling! No! I don't want to fall! Nina! Where are you?

End of prologue.

SCENE ONE

Lights up on FROG. *He is softly singing to himself.*

FROG
"You're not far away. You're not far . . . away. When I miss you . . . I close my eyes . . . I'm sleepy to me . . . I'd like to sleep . . . one time . . . not go anywhere, but just sleep . . . Don't want no visitors either . . . sleep . . . come snag me . . .

[*From upstage* ELAINE *enters. She is an older sister to Frog. She is well dressed.*]

ELAINE
Frog? Brother? Frog.

FROG
Frog's in the buttermilk, shoo frog shoo . . . jay! Let me sleep . . .

ELAINE
Frog!

FROG
Who's there?

ELAINE
Brother, it's me. Your sister Elaine.

FROG
'Lainey? Sis? Is that you, my sister?

[*He struggles to his feet.*]

ELAINE
Listen, brother, listen to me. My son, Elmo, is coming to you.

FROG
Your boy? Your son? My son, I mean, nephew?

ELAINE
Yes. I told him to go to you.

FROG
Is he going to bring his own Spam?

ELAINE
What?

FROG
We don't have much to eat here 'Lainey.

ELAINE
You'll have money and food. You have all that you need.

FROG
Why's he coming here? Don't kids like to go someplace good in the summer?

ELAINE
You have to teach him.

FROG
Tea . . . teach? Me? To sleep?

ELAINE
No. You have to teach him how to dance.

FROG
No. No, not me! No . . .

ELAINE
It's time he learned.

FROG
No. Ask, ask, ask our cousin Kent. Not me. I can't teach. Look it, look it, 'Lainey.

ELAINE
You're my brother. You're Elmo's uncle. You have to do this.

FROG
Yeah, no, I don't know! Look at me! I'm not that way, anymore. No.

ELAINE
What way? What are you talking about?

FROG
I don't dance anymore! All those pretty outfits out there. Who, who would want to see me dance out there?

ELAINE
Frog. There isn't anybody else I can ask.

FROG
They'll laugh at me!

ELAINE
Who? Who will laugh at you?

FROG
You know. Them guys. People. Our people. Different ones, who, who see me. They will laugh at me, and then they'll laugh at him too! All those years I stood and laughed at others, who I thought dressed funny, didn't look right . . . now, now, I'm the one . . . I'm the funny looking one!

ELAINE
Not all of them. They don't laugh at you when you help people out, do they?

FROG
Yes—no—sometimes, I guess but I know I can't teach, teach him.

ELAINE
All you have to do is go to the train depot and meet him. Bring him here, to our home. Teach him here. No one will see you, and no one will laugh at you. And at the celebration, he will dance for us, for all of us. You can show him.

FROG
No. Look it—look at me! I'm, I'm broken. I fell. Remember? Please 'Lainey, please. Sis, don't, don't ask me, okay. Ask, ask someone else? No me, please, sis. Okay, okay, okay, please. I, I, can't teach. Show him what, "leggin' on, leggin' off"?

ELAINE
You have to do this Frog. You are his uncle. My brother. You have to do this.

FROG
I can teach him to, uh, to, uh, make frybread? We can make it right here in the house will no one, no one will see us. Lard in, dough in—done!

ELAINE
No. You're the one to do this. For me, Mom, Dad, and yourself.

FROG
I miss you . . . that man had no right to take you away from us . . .

ELAINE
I'm here. Don't be afraid, Frog. It will turn out all right. You are beautiful to me.

   [*She exits.*]

FROG
Don't lie! I'm not, not pretty! Elaine! 'Lainey? Mess up, mess this up? Hey? Elaine? I don't want to do this.

Blackout. End of scene.

SCENE TWO

Outside of FROG's *house. It is later in the morning.* ELMO *enters. He is wearing street clothes. He searches for a place to hide. Three other kids enter.*

EMERSON
Where'd he go? Huh? Where is he!

DENISE
Don't yell. I don't know. I thought you knew.

EMERSON
Shut up! I bet he has all kinds of money. You didn't see him at all?

NELLIE
No. What part of no don't you understand?

EMERSON
Hey punk! Come on out and laugh at our faces now. "Little Punk!"

[*The kids laugh.* FROG *enters. He stands a few feet from the door of his house, and he holds a broom handle for a cane.*]

FROG
Hey you kids! Get, get away from my house.

EMERSON
Whoa, check out this old fool.

DENISE
Shut up, you old man freak!

FROG
I'll get the cops if you don't leave.

NELLIE
Let's leave the old fool alone.

EMERSON
Don't let him scare you. He won't do anything. He's nothing but an old freak. No one's going to help him. I said . . .

[TYLER *enters. He is a man shaped by hard work.*]

TYLER
He said to get out of his yard, so I'm telling you to get your little brown butts in gear.

EMERSON
We're sorry uncle.

TYLER
If you don't get moving, you will be. You too.

NELLIE
Damn. Let's go.

[EMERSON *stands for a moment and then leaves, followed by the girls.*]

TYLER
Elmo?

[ELMO *stands up and crosses to* TYLER.]

ELMO
Uncle Frog? Where were you? I was waiting for you, but you weren't there. I tried to call for a cab, but you guys don't have taxis out here, not even a commuter bus. I'm glad you're here. You came right in time.

TYLER
Wait. I'm not your uncle Frog.

ELMO
You're not? Well, where is he?

[TYLER *points to* FROG.]

FROG
Hi. Me. I'm, uh, I'm, uh Fr . . . Your uncle Frog. You're Elmo?

ELMO
Yeah. Are you sure you're not my uncle Frog?

FROG
He's Tyler. He's my friend, my buddy.

TYLER
Elmo, I'm Tyler Grant. I've been a friend to your ma and your uncle since we were little.

FROG
Me and Tyler used to dance together. All the times . . .

TYLER
Wish you would come back, Frog. Different ones ask about you.

FROG
Don't need to dance, dance competitions. I have work. Elmo. Nephew. Go inside and rest. Food, I got food in the fridge. I have, I have a phone. Call 'Lainey. Your mom. Tell her, you're here.

ELMO
But my mom is . . . must be the sun. All right.

[*He crosses and enters the house.* FROG *crosses to* TYLER.]

FROG
What, what you think, Tyler? Huh?

TYLER
He has his mom's eyes. Kind of moves like you.

FROG
No, no. You think he can dance?

TYLER
Yeah. Why not? You can too if you would just come out and join your relatives and be a part . . .

FROG
I'm here! They can come and visit me if they want—now. I'm not like that doctor said! I'm not *shnugah*! I can see.

TYLER
You took it pretty hard, Frog. Long time. Be honest. You couldn't go to the station to pick up that boy, enit?

FROG
Indin time! I was on Indin time; his bus was on bus time.

TYLER
Lucky for you those kids chased him all the way from there to your house then, enit?

FROG
It worked out . . . he's here, enit?

TYLER
Yeah, but is he really going to be here?

FROG
His, his hair.

TYLER
What?

FROG
Looks like a rainbow sat on his head.

TYLER
I don't think some of those colors are in a rainbow, or in nature.

FROG
I wonder if, if those colors come off, when he washes his hair?

TYLER
If you want, we can take him swimming and throw him in the river. See what happens.

FROG
No, no. Don't want to harm the fish.

TYLER
Brother, listen to me. I won championships at the Denver Powwow, Gathering of Nations, Red Earth. Let me lead the honor dance for your family. I'll bring you and your family great recognition when the people see me at head of the line. You and I have been dancing all our lives. We are Indin. Nothing bad on this kid, but I don't know if this kid will learn. But I mean, not from just you, but from anybody. You know?

FROG
What, what do you mean? I can, I can teach.

TYLER
Well, I guess you can teach him the basic steps, but don't be expecting to turn him into a champion dancer in the next few days. Look at him Frog. He has never been out of the city. His daddy raised him in the city and made him totally unaware of this life. I bet he didn't even know he was Indin until 'Lainey told him and taught him. Judging from what I've seen so far, those lessons really didn't take hold. I know you want this honor dance to be good for you and your other family members. Why does he have to lead? Do your other family members agree to this? If you weren't so . . . the way you are in your head about this, you could do it. Hell. Let me dance for you.

FROG
Sho, shoot? Me! I'll dance.

TYLER
Good! If you think you can, then do it! Don't mess around about this, Frog. This is serious. This is for all the people here. You can't have some half-breed-looking white boy out there trying to be Indin.

FROG
Gee, Tyler. Why do you say things like that, huh? Huh?

TYLER
Because you know how these people are around here. If they don't say it to your face, they'll always say it behind your back. Besides, the people see this kind of kid at all our ceremonies. These kids don't even know why they're there half the time. I'm talking whites, wannabes, posers, fakes, pretendins! They just want people to see them with Indin people, they sure don't want to be Indin. . . . Ahh! I'm looking out for you, Frog. No one around here will blame you if you have me dance for your family.

FROG
I will. I'll blame myself. Yeah but, but, he's my nephew, and I'm, I'm his dad now, a second dad. That's our way, so, so don't say things like that, okay? Okay, Tyler?

TYLER
Is your head feeling all right, Frog?

FROG
Yeah, yeah. Why?

TYLER
I just wanted to be sure you're not thinking stupid again.

FROG
You, you should go now, Tyler. Before, before you say something, you won't be able to, be able to take back, enit?

TYLER
I tried. People around here make fun of you because of the way you look, and all I'm trying to do is prevent them from laughing at you again for this little white boy. If you are still afraid of dancing and being seen, they'll know it. You can't hide that. You couldn't even go to the station and pick him up. You are going to have to really work, Frog. If you aren't going to do it? I don't know. Remember. I tried to help you people.

[*He exits.*]

FROG
Huh! Too broken, too white, but these are all my relations, enit?

Blackout. End of scene.

SCENE THREE

FROG *and* ELMO *are sitting at the table eating dinner.*

FROG
You, you aren't hungry? I know I am. Mmm, good Spam. It's fresh. I usually don't eat dinner.

ELMO
Uh-huh. Sodium sliders, yum.

FROG
We're coming up on the celebration. We have just a few more days left to get you ready. Do you want to start pretty soon?

ELMO
Start what?

FROG
To, to dance. I don't expect you, you to be doing anything fancy, just, just a few steps, traditional, I think.

ELMO
What?

FROG
Let me see. Uh.

[*Rises and goes to a trunk and begins to drag it to the table.*]

ELMO
You need some help, Uncle Frog?

[FROG *makes several attempts to lift the trunk onto the table.*]

FROG
No, yeah, no. I got it, wait. Yeah, no. Yeah. I need help.

[ELMO *helps* FROG. FROG *opens the trunk.*]

ELMO
What is this?

FROG
What used to be me.

[FROG *produces an old dancing outfit.*]

I know, know it looks kinda' funny, kinda' old, and it, it smells kinda', it kinda' smells, but it was mine. Here. Here. I want you to wear it when you dance for our family, our people.

ELMO
What? What did you say? Hey, "our people?" "Our family?" I barely know you.

FROG
I'm your uncle.

ELMO
All I know is what my mom said. I was just a kid. Who are you?

FROG
I'm her little Froggy . . . Elainey, your mom used to call me that. We both used to dance. Every summer. Our mom and dad would take us to every celebration on the rez. We didn't go to the big ones—once in a while, when we had lease money, we'd go. Fun, fun time, all our relatives, singing and dancing—Celebration! I used to dance in competitions with Tyler. We made a lot of hamburger money back then . . . not just chopped meat.

ELMO
What are you talking about?

FROG
Well, what, different ones, people call powwow circuit.

ELMO
What, what happened to you?

FROG
I, I, I fell.

ELMO
Fall? Off of what? Oh man, I mean, uh . . .

FROG
I look rugged, enit?

ELMO
What? What did you say? "E-nit?"

FROG
You don't know "enit"? Enit? *Aye.*

ELMO
What are you saying, old man?

FROG
Uh, look it, Nephew . . .

ELMO
"Look it"? Is that like enit? I don't understand this. I came here because I didn't want to go back to the white family who adopted me. When I get here, I get harassed by a semi-creepy rez ghetto gang. You say you have a TV, but it is a huge box with wires and no hookups for cable or my games. I can't even get internet here. And now you are talking some language no one I know of uses.

FROG
Sit down. Sit, Nephew. Listen to me. Listen. When, when I was your age. I used to dance all the time, but I made sure to dance every year at this one celebration. It was a, a "powwow"? You know what they call a "powwow"?

ELMO
Yeah. Sort of. I know what it is. My mom used to take me to the Indian socials at the Indian center when I was little.

FROG
Well, I used to dance with Tyler. We would dance every year at this celebration. We didn't dance for contest money, like some do today, but we danced for our relations, and for those who couldn't dance. These celebration would last for four days. Not one day, but for four days, with people from all over; North Dakota, South Dakota, Wyoming, Washington, Idaho, and even from Canada.

One year, that was when I met my wife, Nina. Tyler and me took off our dance outfits and got into our snagging gear, *aye!* We were walking around and stopped to have some coffee. We were standing by the grandstand drinking our coffee, and, and then I saw her.

[NINA *appears at the other side of the stage.*]

It hit me hard. I had to go over here and talk with this pretty one. I didn't ask Tyler to go over to talk with her. I was afraid he'd see her and try to snag her for himself. She's so beautiful. Her smile, made my heart feel funny, good, scary, but really good. I don't even remember how far she was from me once I started walking . . . don't even know if I was walking, *aye!*

[*He does, and as he crosses to her his body returns undamaged.*]

I was real lucky. They had a drum who did a couple's dance. There we are. The youngest ones out here.

[*They start to dance.*]

NINA
Are you shaking?

FROG
No. It's these cowboy boots. The heels feel funny.

NINA
You're wearing tennis shoes.

FROG
I, I danced a lot tonight.

NINA
So I guess you'll be dancing with a lot of girls tonight, huh?

FROG
But only one woman, you.

NINA
Aye! I bet you wouldn't talk that way around my parents, or friends, huh?

FROG
Don't know? Why do your parents need to be talked to this way anyway?

NINA
Ahh! So cute. Settle down or you'll be doing a two-step with one set of legs. Do you like it here, Frog?

FROG
I don't want this to end, sounds foolish, but that's how good this is.

NINA
Then don't stay away. I'll always be here for you.

FROG
What? Where are you . . .

NINA
We are here for you always, Frog. Don't keep yourself from us.

FROG
I don't want to go now. I just . . .

ELMO
What happened? Uncle? Uncle!

[*Music stops and* NINA *exits.*]

FROG
I, I hear you! I don't want to . . . it . . . hard to talk about. Guess. You have to know. One year, we were coming to the celebration. We were

turning from the interstate to the entrance road and I didn't see this semi that sped up and passed a car, and he hit our car. I was thrown from the car. Skidded across the highway. Tore my face in half. Nina, Nina, oh my wife. *Wynin was-tay,* Nina. She died instantly, with our, our only baby we would never hold, or see. Tore my heart in half.

[*He returns to* ELMO *at the table, and as he returns and crosses his body in this world he is restored.*]

I messed up. I'm still falling, from the car, from that night, from Nina . . . I, I will never have those things again. I fell and I'm crooked . . . never gonna have that balanced step . . .

ELMO
Sorry to hear this, Uncle. No one said, or told . . .

FROG
Don't, don't want to talk about it. Nothing good comes from it.

ELMO
How did you, or why do they call you "Frog," Uncle?

FROG
When, when I was in the hospital. My family, they came to visit me. I was all stretched out. They said I looked like a frog. They weren't being mean to me. We tease. They were just trying to bring me back.

ELMO
Did they?

FROG
I guess so. I'm here.

ELMO
Yeah, but do you want to be here?

FROG
Not like this, but mostly, not without Nina. I'm, I'm here though. For you, Nephew?

ELMO
No.

FROG
Why, why not? You're home now. Your people are here.

ELMO
What people? I don't know these "people." You tell me these are my "people"? This is my home? I live with a white couple in the suburbs. We have a dog and an arthritic cat. That's my home. This isn't my home? The "rez"! So far, so far it's been nothing but a big waste. There's nothing fun to do around here. Everything goes to black at five. The TV stations go off the air at midnight. How can anybody enjoy this place?

[*Special light on* FROG. ELMO *freezes.*]

FROG
Now what do I do? I messed up! See, Elaine. I told you.

[ELAINE *appears at the scrim.*]

ELAINE
I've been watching, brother. It looks like to me you haven't done anything.

FROG
Yes, I have! Him. He hasn't . . . I've fed him, two cans of Spam too, more than once too . . .

ELAINE
You have to do this, my brother. For our family.

FROG
But, but, Tyler. Tyler's mad at me. He won't help with this boy.

ELAINE
I'm not asking Tyler. I'm asking you to teach him to dance.

FROG
Tyler's better'n me. He still can dance, and people still look at him and think he's good. He's not broken. He could teach Elmo. Please, Elaine?

ELAINE
Why, my brother?

FROG
Ty, Tyler's not like me. He's, he's not like me.

ELAINE
Tyler's not left-handed, *aye!*

FROG
DON'T MAKE FUN OF ME!

ELAINE
Stop it, Frog! I've had enough of this. Stop looking at the scars on your skin and look what's inside of your skin, beneath the scars. There is something there that Tyler will never have. It's, it's what brought Nina to you. It wasn't because you were a good dancer. She came to you because of your heart. It's why I've sent you my son. I want you to show him how to grow, to be a man. He is beautiful to me, just like you are. Don't listen to your head all the time. Your eyes are lying to your heart. Don't give up.

[*Special fades.* ELMO *is on his feet near* FROG.]

ELMO
And what's with all these dogs without leashes? There are no leash laws. Dogs are running amok, Uncle. Mad dogs and gangs rule these dirt roads and . . . uh, uh, Uncle, you have some medicine you should be taking? Uncle? Uncle?

FROG
Oh? Wha, what? No.

ELMO
I hope you aren't mad about what I've said?

FROG
No. I was, uh, uh, talking with someone.

ELMO
Yeah. Me. So? Uncle?

FROG
What? What, Nephew?

ELMO
Is it all right if I just leave and go back to the city?

FROG
You're already home, Nephew. Listen, Nephew. You want to know who your people are? Where you really live?

ELMO
I think it was easier to trying to piece together what *enit* means. Now what are you talking about, Uncle?

FROG
This dance. All you have to do is do it, just this one time. Just this once. This isn't a competition. No one will be watching your steps, eyeing your outfit. I think your mom will, will, go along with it. Yeah, she'll go along with it.

ELMO
What?

FROG
I've talked with her and she agrees.

ELMO
My mom? You talked with her? Is this another Indian thing? Cool, like the force. She's . . .

FROG
Just this one time, Elmo, my nephew. Just this one time.

ELMO
And then I can leave?

FROG
I promise you. When the celebration comes, and you go out there to dance in the honor song for your grandparents, that's all you will need to do it, just one time.

ELMO
No tricks?

FROG
No.

ELMO
And you're going to teach me? How? Uncle, you can barely walk. I'm going to be in front of all those people who don't even know me, and I'll be looking, looking real sucky.

FROG
What? Stink? I don't know, but I just remembered. I remembered there's more to this than looks.

ELMO
I don't know.

FROG
Either way, you can't leave until after the celebration.

ELMO
I can always find my way back.

FROG
You won't have to look. After, after the celebration, and after the dance.

ELMO
When I dance, you promise I won't look, you know, look like sh . . .

FROG
Better'n . . . better'n I used to. I promise you, Nephew. It's all I got to give you. My word. I promise you, you won't look sad.

ELMO
All right. If that's the only way I'm going to get back to the city. I'll do it.

Blackout. End of scene.

DREAM WORLD SCENE

ELMO *is on the stage sitting in a chair, sleeping. We hear music and the music wakes him. He slowly looks around.*

ELMO
What . . . what is that? Where am I?

[FROG *enters. He is dancing.*]

FROG
Come on, Nephew. Come dance with us.

[FROG *continues to dance in a circle and behind him are two* DANCERS *in Warcraft costumes. Following the* WARCRAFT DANCERS *is* ELAINE.]

ELMO
Mom! Mom, is that?

FROG
Come and join us Elmo.

[*The* WARCRAFT DANCERS *cross over to* ELMO.]

ELMO
I can't dance.

FROG
Sure, you can. All Indins know how to dance. Come on.

[*ELMO tries to get out of the chair, and the* WARCRAFT DANCERS *place the black cloth on him.* ELMO *gets up, but now shares the damaged body of* FROG.]

ELMO
Help me! Mom! Uncle Frog! Help me! I can't dance.

FROG
You can do it. Come on. Join us.

[ELMO *tries to move and falls.*]

ELMO
Help me!

FROG
Come on, Nephew.

[ELMO *struggles some more.* ELAINE *disappears.*]

ELMO
Mom. Help me!

FROG
Don't give up, Nephew. Come on and dance.

ELMO
I can't do it! I don't know how to dance.

WARCRAFT DANCERS
Why not? All Indians know how to dance! We're of the Warcraft World. Even we know how to dance. Eat more hot pockets and see what happens. All Indians can dance! They have to dance! To be Indian you have to dance!

ELMO
I'm Indian. I can do it!

WARCRAFT DANCERS
Then do it! Dance! Dance Elmo! Come on!

ELMO
I can't. Someone help me!

[ELMO *struggles to move, but can't.*]

Blackout.

SCENE FOUR

FROG *and* ELMO *are outside of the house.*

ELMO
I thought you said this was going to be easy, Uncle Man?

FROG
It was, is, when I was young and . . . young.

ELMO
Why's this dance so special, Uncle?

FROG
It's for your grandparents. Our way of thanking them and giving them respect. You might not remember them. You were just a baby then. A little guy.

ELMO
I don't remember being here.

FROG
Yeah. You were here. When your mom set you down on the floor you kept all the bugs in their place.

ELMO
How'd I do that?

FROG
Like this.

[*He demonstrates* ELMO *eating the bugs.*]

I bet they tasted just like chicken, enit, Nephew?

ELMO
I did that?

FROG
McBug-licious.

ELMO
Uncle? How long has it been since you've seen my mom?

FROG
A few days ago.

ELMO
Is this that Indian "force" thingy again? Okay. She was here? In your house?

FROG
No. No. I don't mean like that.

ELMO
Oh? I know this is going to be complicated, but what do you mean?

FROG
I just closed my eyes.

ELMO
You have her tattooed on your eyelids?

FROG
No. That's not funny, Nephew.

ELMO
I'm going to . . .

FROG
Fridge. Get me a glass of water, please, Nephew?

ELMO
Yeah.

[ELMO *begins to exit and is stopped by* TYLER. TYLER *stares* ELMO *down.* ELMO *hurries off.*]

TYLER
Frog.

FROG
Okay, okay, okay. I'm doing the best I can, Sis . . .

TYLER
Frog! It's me.

FROG
What?

[FROG *sits up.*]

TYLER
Laying down on the job, huh?

FROG
What, what you want?

TYLER
I came by to visit.

FROG
Oh. I'll have that boy get you . . .

TYLER
No. That's all right. I don't want anything.

FROG
Hot, hot afternoon, enit?

TYLER
Yeah. I was in town the other day and saw Emmy and her kids.

FROG
How is she?

TYLER
She's fine. She had all her grandkids with her. She was buying them some ice cream.

FROG
Make me wish. Ice cream. Oh. Yeah?

TYLER
She's on the celebration committee this year, you know that?

FROG
So, what did you say to her? Did, did you tell her you were going to dance for my parents in their honor dance?

TYLER
What? You . . . No. I thought you had already done that.

FROG
I, I can't. My nephew Elmo is going to dance.

TYLER
Frog! He can't even walk the dance. You don't dance anymore because you're all crippled up in your head. I've been watching you two this morning.

FROG
Oh. That's, that's what that smell is.

TYLER
Trying to be funny too, huh? Frog. You remember Eldon Rose's little boy, Hank?

FROG
No. No. I'm not going to ask him to dance.

TYLER
No. I'm not-stupid again, huh? All right. Look, do you remember him, or not?

FROG
Yeah.

TYLER
He won his first competition when he was only ten. He was dancing here with us when he was a little guy.

FROG
So?

TYLER
That's because Eldon's boy is from here. He's one of us. Not like this kid. You don't know it, but in the end, you are going to really embarrass that kid.

FROG
How? That's, that's the last thing . . .

TYLER
People will see it even though you can't.

FROG
Tyler, what happened to you? Huh? I thought you were a friend?

TYLER
I am. You and I will be here. This kid will pack his bags and leave right after the celebration, and it will be the last time we'll see him. I called around and heard this boy was in a lot of trouble back there. Ever since his mother, well, he has been a big problem. His adopted parents were glad to get rid of him. You watch and see.

FROG
He's, he's Elaine's boy. He might not be your boy, but he's my son.

TYLER
Then be a good father, Frog, and do the right thing. Don't do this to that kid.

[ELMO *enters carrying two plastic tumblers.*]

Think about it, Frog. Everyone at the celebration will be laughing at you and the kid. If you don't want to do it for yourself, or this kid, then do it for your family.

ELMO
Hey, thanks for all of your support, really, man.

[TYLER *exits*.]

ELMO
Here you go, Uncle. What did he want?

FROG
Oh. Nothing. He just wanted to show me something, I guess. Ready to go again?

ELMO
Uncle Frog? How, how bad do I look?

FROG
Better'n me.

ELMO
Really?

FROG
No. I just don't want to get you down. You're getting better, Elmo. It's going to get better.

ELMO
Uncle? Why couldn't you just do it? You know how to dance. Why don't you do it?

FROG
Yeah, yeah. I know how to do it.

ELMO
Then show me a few moves, Uncle.

[ELMO *starts a tape on an old cassette recorder.*]

Come on, Uncle.

FROG
No. You need to learn, not . . .

ELMO
Just a few steps, not an entire dance.

[FROG *slowly starts to dance. His footsteps are awkward but once he finds the movement of the beat his footwork is steadier.*]

Nice, Uncle.

[FROG *starts to do a little more complicated move with his body. He falls, hard.*]

FROG
No! I knew it! No!

ELMO
Uncle. I'm here.

FROG
I knew it! I told them, I'd fall.

ELMO
You're all right, Uncle. I have you. Come on.

FROG
See. I said, I said—No! I can't do it.

ELMO
Uncle, come on. Let me help you up!

FROG
No one listens! No one hears you when you're like me!

ELMO
I hear you, Uncle. Please. Uncle? Are there medicines I should get for you?

FROG
You have to do it. You have to do it.

ELMO
What, Uncle? Get your medicines?

FROG
No. Dance. You. Nephew Elmo. You.

ELMO
Here, here, Uncle. Here's your stick.

[FROG *is now standing.*]

FROG
Wait. Wait. Let me catch my breath.

ELMO
There's nothing broken right, Uncle? You didn't break anything?

FROG
Already did, but nothing now.

ELMO
I was, I was kind of hoping you could do it, Uncle?

FROG
Really? You hate it this much?

ELMO
No. I don't hate it. I don't understand it. There are a lot of things I don't understand. For you, but not for me. I still can't find an answer for myself. All I have are a bunch of words that are supposed to be Indin and I don't even understand. *Enit, look-it,* or why you guys say *jokes* when it's obvious it is a joke.

FROG
You're doing this dance, because I don't have kids.

ELMO
And that's the only reason?

FROG
It's, it's a real big reason.

ELMO
I don't understand it. Uncle? I don't know if I'm "Indin." I don't really know what that means. There are other kids at my school who say they're Indian, they have a great grandmother who was a princess, or they are some distant relative to Pocahontas, but they don't know what it means. Look at how I'm dressed. Are these the traditional clothes of our people? I don't think so. How am I supposed to look, talk, think, be? You haven't answered these questions?

FROG
I would say like me, but I don't want to scare you, *aye*.

ELMO
What are you saying? Is what you're saying Indian? All of it? If it is, I don't get it.

FROG
No. Sometimes, I'm thinking in ways I shouldn't be.

ELMO
So, if I do this dance. This will make me Indian?

FROG
I don't know. In a way it would.

ELMO
I thought if I came out of here. It would be a great way for me to see something else. I didn't come here to be an "Indin." I came here to see where my mom grew up, and maybe myself. Whatever that might be? I think I just might leave.

[ELMO *exits.*]

FROG
I messed up again, Elaine.

Blackout. End of scene.

SCENE FIVE

FROG *sits at the table, in and out of sleep.*

FROG
I messed up Elaine.

[ELAINE *appears from behind a screen and crosses to the table and sits.*]

ELAINE
No you didn't, brother.

FROG
Why is he always asking me about being Indin? Doesn't he know? I'm his uncle, your brother, you are my sister, he is your son, he is my nephew, and we are Indins, and so is he. That, that isn't so hard.

ELAINE
It's a lot different away from home, Frog.

FROG
He should just move here then. He should be here and be an Indin with me. You know, 'Lainey? I wish you were here. Don't leave me here, alone.

ELAINE
I'm always here, brother. It's important Elmo has a home here. He needs it more now than ever. I want to make sure he knows who he is. To know what he is. I'm so proud of you. You're doing good. I know Nina would be proud of you.

FROG
Really?

ELAINE
Look. Ask her.

[*She motions to the screen and* NINA *appears.*]

Go to her, brother.

FROG
Nina? I hope no one wakes me up, boy. Uh, is, is that . . . my heart? Nina.

[*He tries to cross to her. He falls halfway to her.*]
Nina! I can't . . .

NINA
Don't quit, husband. Please. Don't give up. You can make it.

[*He gets to his feet and crosses to her. As he crosses to her, his body returns to his "younger self."*]

FROG
Nina. My wife . . . I, I've missed. . . .

[NINA *motions him to be silent. The music begins, and she takes him by the hand and they start to dance.*]

Nina, I want to live here with you forever.

NINA
I'm all right, my husband. It's time for you to be with me. It's time for just us.

[*They continue to dance in silence. Two lights appear. They are the headlights of an advancing truck.* FROG *begins to panic. He grabs* NINA *tightly as the lights become brighter. The lights over take them.* FROG *screams. They stand in silence for a moment and then he slowly releases his grip.*]

I'm still here. I didn't leave you, my husband. I never have.

FROG
Come, come back with me? Please?

NINA
No. I'm here.

FROG
I want you closer, come join me in my world, please.

NINA
I can't go with you.

FROG
Then, then let me come with you then? Please? Don't leave me behind, alone.

NINA
You can't. You have something to do here. Finish it. I'll wait. We will all be here for you.

FROG
If I were different, didn't fall, didn't fall out of my body, and was the way I once was. With you I was balanced out, but now I'm all crooked. I won't mess up so . . .

NINA
You're not messing up. Just go back and finish this. Remember, it's not you, it's for your parents. Our parents, and others.

FROG
I don't want to leave you.

NINA
I left you, but not by choice. I'm here for you. Just be patient and wait. When it is time. I'm here. I won't let you fall out of yourself. If you ever do, I'll catch you and pour you right back into yourself. Don't be afraid to live. I don't want you to be this way . . . So let go of your fear and be strong for yourself and our nephew—your new son. Now, close your eyes and hold me, my husband.

[*Music starts back up and they continue their dance.*]

Blackout. End of scene.

SCENE SIX

Night. ELMO *is sound asleep in a small cot.* FROG *is asleep in a rundown easy chair. He is covered with a faded star quilt.* ELMO *starts to stir. He jumps out of cot standing straight up.*

ELMO
Ow! Fuck! Ow! Uncle! Uncle!

[*He is nearly falling over.* FROG *struggles to get up.*]

Uncle!

FROG
What's wrong, Nephew? What's wrong?

ELMO
My leg! Oh man! It hurts!

[FROG *makes his way to* ELMO.]

This has never happened before. What is it?

[FROG *examines* ELMO*'s calf.*]

FROG
It's nothing, Nephew. Just a Charley horse.

ELMO
What is that? An Indin thing?

FROG
No. Leg cramp. From all the dancing you've been doing, but you haven't been drinking any water lately, enit?

ELMO
It hurts!

FROG
Here, here, I'll take care of it.

[FROG *begins to rub the soreness of the leg.*]

It, it'll be gone soon.

ELMO
Is this going to happen every time I dance?

FROG
No. Your legs will get use to it. It happened now because you aren't used to this kind of activity, and you haven't been drinking any water. Better, Nephew?

ELMO
Yeah. Thanks.

FROG
Don't sit down yet. Here. You continue to rub it.

[FROG *stands. He crosses the room and turns on a light.*]

ELMO
When can I sit?

FROG
When it tells you. Here. Let me see.

[FROG *moves* ELMO's *hands out of the way and sees scars on* ELMO's *wrists and forearms.*]

Nephew? Who did this to you?

ELMO
No one. I did it.

FROG
Why?

ELMO
What's wrong? Indians aren't supposed to do things like this?

FROG
No. That's not why.

ELMO
I did these things because I wasn't feeling good about things, me, mainly.

FROG
Does your mom know?

ELMO
She knows. She got me into a treatment center right away when I first started to do it. It was her second husband, Derek.

FROG
Your dad?

ELMO
He's not my dad. He didn't care. He said I was too weak. "Damn Indians are too weak," is what he'd say. He called me a loser. Son of a squaw is what he would say. Then my mom finally divorced him.

FROG
Nephew—

ELMO
You ever see this before, Uncle?

[FROG *nearly shrinks. He slowly raises his arm and rolls up his shirt sleeve to reveal several old scars.*]

FROG
When Nina, my wife, left this world. I wanted to follow her.

ELMO
Did anyone call you a loser?

FROG
No.

ELMO
If my dad were here, he would call us both losers.

FROG
You aren't a loser, Nephew. I fell, and you need a place to land. When you do, I wish it's here.

ELMO
I don't know what you mean, Uncle? Is that some Indian belief? My father, after the second time I went in, he tried to make it up to me by taking me to a Redskins football game. He said it was his way of bringing me closer to my people. When I told my mom, she got mad and argued with him. He hit her. She didn't leave him then. Is that an Indian thing, Uncle? To take that kind of abuse and not say anything? My father said he did it to knock the Indian out of her. Is that true?

FROG
No. We never honor the abuse of our women. Derek is a *wasicu*. He knows nothing of your mom or us.

ELMO
You know what, Uncle? I saw her . . . I saw her body. When the police came it was the light of their cars and ambulance that woke me up. I felt so mad that I didn't wake up to help her. I should have helped her, and I couldn't even wake the fuck up. I was just as bad as him . . . I was so angry at her . . . I thought it made me like him. Then am I going to be that way? Or something worse, because I don't know. I don't know anything.

FROG
No, Nephew. You aren't going to be like him. You'll be much different.

ELMO
What? An Indian? I mean, I always heard that Indians dance and I thought that was a stereotype and here I am, learning to dance.

FROG
No. I'll teach you the reason. Reason why we do, reason why we are who we are, reason why we live.

ELMO
When? I want to know now. This is a waste of time. I keep on hearing it's going to get better, and it never does. I made a mistake coming out here. It's nothing but a lie!

[ELMO *runs off.*]

FROG
Elmo . . . Nephew . . . 'Lainey . . . I mess this up real good, enit?

Blackout. End of scene.

SCENE SEVEN

In front of a store. ELMO *lies on the pavement and is badly beaten.*

EMERSON
Beat his ass good! Check to see if he has anything else.

DENISE
Didn't think we'd catch you, bitch! Stop looking at me!

NELLIE
No more money. Just this lame ass iPhone. This is it.

DENISE
I'm not done with him yet. Get up, white boy. The way he's lookin' at me.

[*Kicks* ELMO.]

Come on.

[TYLER *enters. He walks over to the kids. The kids freeze.* TYLER *looks down at* ELMO.]

ELMO
Help me, please, Uncle Tyler?

EMERSON
He made fun of how we are.

NELLIE
He keeps looking at me.

TYLER
Get out of here. Go on!

[*The* KIDS *walk off.*]

ELMO
Uncle Ty . . . Tyler . . .

TYLER
I'm not your uncle. How does it feel to be Indin? You were doing the right thing, but now I need to know. Do you want to get on the bus? Go to your uncle's home, or go to the hospital and then go back? Because, you don't belong here.

[TYLER *lifts* ELMO *up.*]

Blackout. End of scene.

SCENE EIGHT

[ELMO *lies motionless on the steps of* FROG's *house.* FROG *is holding* ELMO.]

ELMO
I fell.

FROG
Yeah. We all do, once in a while, but, but look where you landed, Nephew.

ELMO
Uncle?

FROG
Can, can you get up? Here. Let me help you. No, wait, wait, I think it would be better if you would just lie still.

[ELMO *rises into a sitting position.*]

ELMO
Damn. I must be broke? Enit?

[*Goes back down.*]

FROG
You know how to say it now. Good. I, uh, Nephew. I, I'm so . . . I . . .
ELMO
Better get help.

FROG
I called. They're sending an ambulance from the agency. Don't know why Tyler didn't take you there.

ELMO
He gave me choices; bus, city, or here.

FROG
So, so, you wanted to be here? Your home? With your family, huh?

ELMO
Yes. I can't dance, now, huh?

FROG
No. You'll be laid up for a few days, but I, I can do this. I'll do it for our family, Nephew. You know what else, Nephew? Man, you look rugged, Nephew. Maybe I should have taught you a few fighting moves as well. Like that Karate Kid kid. Tripe in, tripe out, *aye!*

ELMO
Feel, feel rugged too.

FROG
Nephew? Do you know who did this to you?

ELMO
Some of our people. Guess I'm Indin now?

FROG
No. This means you're American now. You survive it means you're Indin.

[ELMO *coughs and blood pours out.*]

ELMO
Uncle. Uncle.

FROG
Lay still, Nephew, be still.

ELMO
I don't want to die.

FROG
Me too! I don't want you to die either, but you just fell. I know how to get back up. I'll show you. It, it gets easier at different times. It'll—don't cry, my boy.

ELMO
The first time I broke a board with my head.

FROG
I, I broke a mirror once with my face, *aye!*

ELMO
Don't, please don't say things like that about yourself, Uncle. They aren't true. Especially, especially to me.

FROG
I know, I know, it's not true. I'm just trying to make you feel better.

ELMO
You don't have too. I'm here. Uncle, my mom . . .

FROG
She's coming?

ELMO
No. My mom said, said you are a handsome man.

FROG
Aye. You'll have to learn to tease better . . .

ELMO
She was right. She said we are a beautiful people.

FROG
We are, Nephew. No matter how long, or how deep we fall. We are. Don't talk now. Let me tell you the story of how this white man came to our people and to make us Christians. We all sat in his tent. One by one we got up and went to stand in front of him. He touched us on our forehead and said, "The holy ghost passes through you." I was next and when he touched me I let out a loud fart and my cousin Virgil said, "Ho-smokes, Frog. Half of heaven and hell just passed through you." . . . Nephew? Don't go. . . .

Blackout. End of scene.

SCENE NINE

FROG *is wearing his best clothes—a tattered and faded "ribbon shirt," old moccasins with small pieces of duct tape, faded jeans. He stands near the "grand entry" place and dancers walk by him. The* DANCERS' *outfits are bright, colorful, carefully made.* FROG *avoids eye contact as dancers pass him.*

FROG
Ew-shi-gah, I'm so *ew-shi-gah*. No, no . . .

[*An elderly man,* FROG's *grandfather,* ERVIN BIRD, *approaches* FROG, *holding a paper sack.*]

ERVIN
Frog. *Tu-ku-zah*, look at me. Here.

[FROG *looks at him up and down.*]

No! Not at my feet. Here, at me, grandson.

[FROG *looks at him.*]

You're dancing for your folks today. I want to thank you for doing this wonderful thing. I want you to have this. Wear it. It is from me and your grandma. She couldn't make it today, your grandma Fredia. She told me to make sure you get this. Here.

[ERVIN *holds an elk hide vest with elaborate quill work. He helps* FROG *put on the vest.*]

So good you have come back to us, Grandson.

[*From the crowd of* DANCERS, TYLER *enters. He is dressed in full fancy dance regalia. Eagle feather bustles, beaded gauntlets, arm bands, and moccasins.*]

FROG
Thank you, Grandpa.

TYLER
Hello, Frog. Nice vest.

FROG
Yes.

TYLER
I'm sorry to hear what happened to your nephew. How is he doing?

FROG
Alive. He's going to try to make it out here.

TYLER
Yeah? To do what? Dance?

FROG
Don't you laugh, Tyler.

TYLER
Frog. Brother. I'm still willing—

FROG
No. You can go now.

TYLER
Frog. For our relatives—

FROG
Go back in the line . . . right after the relatives. Work your way up again.

[*A cousin*, MINA FLYNN, *enters holding a yellow bundle. She glares down at* TYLER.]

MINA
Cousin, Froggy, Cousin. I'm happy you've come back. Here, for you.

[FROG *unwraps the bundle and removes a pair of white buckskin gauntlets with beadwork down to the fingers.*]

FROG
Pinamiya, Cousin.

[TYLER *turns his back as* MINA *continues to glare at him.*]

TYLER
Frog?

[TYLER *faces* FROG. *They are silent and* TYLER *leaves.*]

MC ANNOUNCER
All right folks. We are going to have a special for this afternoon. The family has asked Blue Feather to sing their honor song for their parents' grand entry. We'll do that in a little while. If you want to—if you're hungry, go over to one of the concessions stand and get yourself something to drink or eat. They have pony paws, Indin tacos, corn soup, and the all-time favorite, pup in a cup. *Aye!* Blue Feather, boys get ready. Jumps the Ground special coming up at ten in Indin Standard Time and counting; 30, 70—*aye!*

[FROG *is trying to steady himself. Next to him is* ELMO *in a wheelchair.*]

ELMO
Look pretty good, Uncle.

FROG
Nephew! Really? Nephew? You didn't, didn't—

ELMO
No. I'm here.

FROG
How'd you manage to get here?

ELMO
In the IHS hospital there was an Indi—cousin next door to me. Her nephews came to visit. They saw me and popped in my room and asked me who I was, who my relatives are. Then one of them said, "Dude, your folks are having that honoring this afternoon. You want to go?" So, they got a wheelchair and snuck me out. Here I am.

FROG
You okay to be here?

ELMO
Yeah. I wish my mom were here.

[FROG *pushes the wheelchair to face the entrance.*]

FROG
See, Nephew. You see all these people. These are your relatives. They carry a part of your mom . . . my Nina . . . they are here with us. What's wrong Elmo?

ELMO
I can't dance so, I won't be Indian.

FROG
You come with me. Look straight ahead. When, Oyate see, they will know you are a part of them and they are a part of you. No dancing, no fancy costume, no beads; just your heart.

MC ANNOUNCER
All right. Blue Feather. Honor song for Vera and Elmo Jumps the Ground special. *Hok-a-hay!* Leading the Jumps the Ground family into our dance arena is . . . uh, their grandson and nephew, Elmo Blaine. Followed by his uncle, Tobias "Frog" Jumps the Ground. Please stand.

> [*The drumbeat starts and then the singers follow.* FROG *struggles pushing* ELMO's *wheelchair. From the groups of dancers, two men's traditional-style cross over to* FROG. *One steadies* FROG, *the other pushes* ELMO's *wheelchair. As they start the arch of a circle other* DANCERS *walk over to* ELMO *and* FROG *and shake their hands and fall in behind them. Slowly a small line forms. Different* DANCERS *enter and the small line becomes a river of people.*]

Blackout. End of play.

Falling Distance

Characters

ADAM, a young man
INK, an uncle to Adam, ageless
SHIYO, a young woman
THOMIE, an aunt to SHIYO, ageless

SCENE ONE

ADAM *is onstage. He is standing on a chair. He looks around and extends his arms outward.*

ADAM
I think, yeah, this is it.

    [INK *enters.*]

I fell.

INK
Fall.

ADAM
And then I felt.

INK
You fell.

ADAM
I know that, but what I'm talking about is different from what you're thinking.

INK
You didn't fall?

ADAM
I fell, but I'm not thinking the way you are.

INK
Good. That was getting old.

ADAM
I was trying to remember what I felt.

INK
When you fell?

ADAM
Yeah, when I fell.

INK
So, what did you feel when you fell?

ADAM
That's what I'm trying to remember. How I felt when I fell.

INK
I fell once.

ADAM
I know. You've told me. Several times and more.

INK
What makes you so sure you're not falling? I mean, right now?

ADAM
You're here.

INK
Are you sure? I'm not sure.

ADAM
Come here, Uncle Ink.

INK
What?

[*Hits* INK *on the head.*]

ADAM
Yeah. You're here.

INK
You're not supposed to treat your relatives like this. Who raised you? Huh?

ADAM
You are, for now.

INK
Oh yeah, enit? I forgot. Get down from there, Nephew, you might fall.

ADAM
Does she think of me?

INK
No.

ADAM
How do you know?

INK
How do you know?

ADAM
I can feel her.

INK
Yeah—there.

ADAM
No, Uncle, here.

[*Points to his heart.*]

INK
You really miss her, enit?

ADAM
Yes, Uncle. I miss her, hunger for her, and sing for her. I would die for her.

INK
History is a very odd thing, Nephew. You have the kind that is written and is based on what people think they've done, or what they could've done. And then there is the spoken kind. It's when people remember what they hear, or what they did, because it comes from the tongue, and from their heart.

ADAM
I want to be with Shiyo. Would you help me, Uncle?

INK
Help you how?

ADAM
Take me to her. Or bring her here to me?

INK
I'm glad you ask me for the simple things of life. I don't know, Nephew? It sounds rough. What if she's full and doesn't have the same hunger like you? Then what, Nephew?

ADAM
She knows me, Uncle. She will always know me.

INK
This isn't good. Do you remember that night, or how you got here?

ADAM
I held her in my arms, and when we kissed, the sky roared and lightning flashed. It was like . . .

INK
Bad stomach? Are you sure it was thunder and lightning? Lightning has a smell to it. Smells better than me.

ADAM
All I could smell was her beauty.

INK
Maybe that's what I should have told my first wife, "It's my beauty you're smelling, honey."

ADAM
And I fell. I fell for a long time. I came here. Where ever this is supposed to be?

INK
And I found you.

ADAM
Yes. Now help me find her.

INK
Is that what you were doing standing up there with your arms out?

ADAM
I fell downward. I thought I could fly up and reach her.

INK
Are you sure we aren't up, and she is the one down below?

ADAM
Yes.

INK
So young—too young. How, how do you know that, Adam?

ADAM
I feel her, Uncle Ink.

INK
Adam, my nephew, I don' know . . .

ADAM
Please? Please, Uncle?

INK
Ah, all right. Let's get your brain going, and you'll think of something.

ADAM
I think if I work my arms like a sparrow . . .

[*Falls down.*]

INK
Nephew? Nephew? Are you all right? Sit down, my boy.

ADAM
It was the darkness again. It was like a large rush from the river, but it was all black. It almost took me again.

INK
Maybe we should be worried about teaching you how to swim, instead of learning to fly, enit?

ADAM
You will help me, Uncle?

INK
Yes, Adam. How do we get her here to you, or you there to her?

ADAM
I'll fly to her.

INK
We need to get you some wings then, enit? Hey? Where would we put them though?

ADAM
My shoulders?

INK
That's one place.

ADAM
Don't go there, Uncle.

INK
Where I was thinking, if we feed you a bunch of beans, you would be like one of those jet thingies.

ADAM
You're bad.

INK
Yeah, but I'm the only one who's helping you! How bad can I . . . I'll be back.

ADAM
Don't get mad and walk off. Where are you going? What are you going to do?

INK
I'm not. I'm going to see who'll loan me some wings. You stay here, because, because that's all about you can do is stay here. I'll be right back. I'm going to do this without getting pecked to death.

Blackout. End of Scene.

SCENE TWO

SHIYO *is standing in front of large round mirror. There are two chairs and a trunk in the space.*

SHIYO
Why you? Why did you come into my world, Adam? Do you think of me as much as I think of you? Are you like all the rest? A bunch of empty words? I wish you were here with me. I miss you, Adam.

[THOMIE *enters. She carries a small travel bag.*]

THOMIE
Shiyo. My girl. Are you ready? We have to be ready when your auntie Grace gets here. You'll like her house. She finally got rid of that man. It'll be better for you there. You won't have time to . . . Oh, my girl.

SHIYO
What? What's wrong, Auntie Thomie?

THOMIE
You're still thinking of him, enit?

SHIYO
So? There's nothing wrong with that.

THOMIE
My girl, for all these years that he's been gone, and, still, you are thinking of him, of that one? It isn't right.

SHIYO
I miss him, Auntie.

THOMIE
I know, my girl.

SHIYO
Haven't you ever felt that way about someone?

THOMIE
A long time ago, when I was your age, too. I know it's hard to move on, but you have to do it.

SHIYO
Sometimes, I can feel him near me.

THOMIE
Even after your uncle Frank came through your room? He worked in here for two days.

SHIYO
Maybe, Auntie, maybe because it isn't bad.

THOMIE
I think it's mean. Making you feel this way all the time. He should just let go, or at least you should.

SHIYO
I don't want him to.

THOMIE
While we're gone I should have your Uncle Frank come through the house one more time for good measure.

SHIYO
That won't change things. I changed when I met Adam, Auntie. I have never been able to go back to the way I was, and I don't want too.

THOMIE
Your mother asked me to watch you and to take care of you. She'll say, "Woman, look how good of a job you've done in taking care of my baby girl," if she sees you are still this way. None of us want you to change, life does.

SHIYO
Does it really look that bad, Auntie?

THOMIE
Yes, Shiyo, it is. It has been nearly four years since that night. We thought you would be feeling different by now. You would be willing to move on with your life. I have never come across something this bad.

SHIYO
It isn't bad, Auntie. I'm in love. How bad is that supposed to be?

THOMIE
Your hair is starting to come back. It looks so pretty, my girl. I remember what it's like to feel this way for someone. How strong it feels. I felt like I walked without stepping, breathing without taking in a breath. It really is a strong feeling. Shiyo? Is this how you feel, my girl?

SHIYO
Yes.

THOMIE
Eww! I feel sorry for you.

SHIYO
Why?

THOMIE
You remind me of your cousin Skin. He walks around town behaving like this, but he gets his feelings from a different source.

SHIYO
That's mean, Auntie. Comparing me to a drunk.

THOMIE
Well, maybe not the same, but the feeling is just as bad. Skin is your uncle. Don't call him that. I need you to wake up from this and to get ready. We're going to the mountains to be with your auntie. We'll stay there for the rest of the summer, so Housing can finish fixing my house. Better to have it done now than the winter. It'll be cooler in the mountains anyways. Do you have everything you want to take with you?

SHIYO
Yes.

THOMIE
Why are you always looking in the mirror, my girl?

SHIYO
Sometimes, sometimes, I feel him standing next to me when I look in the mirror. I can feel how warm his smile is. I smile back at him.

THOMIE
I should have your Uncle Frank take it away.

SHIYO
No. Please don't, Auntie.

THOMIE
Listen to me Shiyo. My girl. This isn't right. You have to let go of this. You have to live, and to do this you have to let go of him.

SHIYO
It was at the powwow.

THOMIE
Yes. He was taken away from us; so was Dinty St. Jormain.

SHIYO
Don't say his name, Auntie?

THOMIE
Who's? Dinty?

SHIYO
Yes. I don't want to hear that name. What a stupid name to give a child.

THOMIE
His parents seemed to like it.

SHIYO
An old stink funny name. Don't say it any more, please, Auntie?

THOMIE
Adam, Dinty, they are both men.

SHIYO
Don't compare the two of them.

THOMIE
Why not? They're just men, or I should say, "barely" men, so young. They want the same thing.

SHIYO
Auntie! How can you say things like that?

THOMIE
Oh, my girl, but I've lived longer than you and I know how men are. They say such sweet things and do the worst things to you. A promise and a lie are one in the same for some of these men. Don't be fooled by them.

SHIYO
Was Uncle this way, too?

THOMIE
He was the worst. He would say one thing and do the other. We all thought he was very funny in his ways. He would promise he wouldn't say this and say it. He would promise never to do that and would wind up doing it. Maybe he hit his head when he was young and no one knew about it. Maybe all these men have bumps on their heads. I'll check your cousin when we get to your auntie's house. Come on. Get your things.

SHIYO
Adam isn't that way.

THOMIE
Maybe, but who will say?

SHIYO
I do, Auntie Thomie. Don't our words count for anything? Why do we always have to believe what we're told? I can tell the difference between a lie and the truth. You can too. We know what is real and what isn't. Are our men so arrogant to believe we can't see what they are doing, when they say they're not? Adam told me that he loved me. He wasn't lying. He didn't even try to touch me. He listened to me. He listened to me, and I listened to him. There wasn't any playing.

THOMIE
Don't get upset, Shiyo, but by holding on to him this way, is this a lie?

SHIYO
I know this is true, Auntie. He loves me.

THOMIE
All right, all right. Maybe I'm wrong. Maybe we are the lie.

SHIYO
Everything happened so fast that night. He's gone. No one found him. They still can't find him.

THOMIE
Do you know where he is, Shiyo?

SHIYO
Yes. I've been trying to tell you. I know where he is.

THOMIE
Let's call the agency then, or at least his relatives.

SHIYO
No. It isn't that way, Auntie. I can't tell you. I don't know the words for it. They won't understand my—me—no.

THOMIE
No? Why not? It would put an end to all this craziness. You should tell someone.

SHIYO
I've been trying to tell you, but I don't have the words.

THOMIE
Come here, my girl.

SHIYO
Why?

THOMIE
I want to feel your head for bumps.

SHIYO
Auntie!

THOMIE
Well, then, feel my head for bumps. One of us should look. Oh, I'm just teasing you, my girl.

SHIYO
I don't like you making fun of me.

THOMIE
I'm not, but you're so young and you sound so serious, but not in a different way and it makes your mom and me nervous.

SHIYO
I heard thunder and saw lightning.

THOMIE
What else?

SHIYO
He fell.

THOMIE
Where did he land then?

SHIYO
I don't know.

THOMIE
You saw him fall, but you didn't see him land? What happened to him? Did something pick him up and carry him away?

SHIYO
No. There were just the two of us.

THOMIE
No other sounds, smells, or movement?

SHIYO
He fell, and then I felt this rush of darkness.

THOMIE
A rush of darkness? From the sky?

SHIYO
I know this sounds strange, Auntie, but it was like the time when we went to the coast, and we watched the big waves come to the shore. This big wave came to us.

THOMIE
You told this to the ones who asked, enit?

SHIYO
To everybody when I was asked, and everybody asked me.

THOMIE
Huh, so strange. Well, get your things together and bring them to the kitchen. As soon as your auntie shows up we'll leave. Getting you away from here might change things for you.

SHIYO
Yes, Auntie. You know what, Auntie? I will still love him.

THOMIE
I love my old man too, my girl, but it's in a different way, a different world. I love you, my girl.

SHIYO
I love you too, Auntie.

[THOMIE *exits.* SHIYO *returns to the mirror.*]

Where did you go Adam? Why don't you answer me? I stand here waiting for you, and only you. I feel so sad that you are not standing here with me. One day, we will stand here looking at one another, without this mirror.

[*She takes a travel bag and exits.* INK *appears from behind the trunk.*]

INK
Whew! I have to cut back on eating meat. Some of my relations live on eating grass and roots, and some of them smoke grass and roots. Hey! This will do it. Nephew's got wings.

[*He takes the mirror.*]

Blackout. End of scene.

SCENE THREE

ADAM *and* INK *are standing in front of the mirror examining it.*

ADAM
These are some strange wings, Uncle.

INK
Well, when I took it, I had an idea, but now I can't remember what it is?

ADAM
Where did you get this? I've been searching for a long time for something and I can't find anything.

INK
Found it.

ADAM
Uncle, I don't mean to be rude, but you didn't take this?

INK
Steal it?

ADAM
Borrowed it, without asking?

INK
No, I didn't ask to borrow it.

ADAM
Steal it?

INK
Nah, took it, is more like it. Negotiated for it.

ADAM
What? Are there others here? Hello! My name is Adam. I'm looking for a way . . .

INK
No! Not here. Not this place! There's just you and me.

ADAM
Well, who—and where—did you get it from?

INK
She wasn't using it.

ADAM
You saw her? You saw Shiyo? When? Where?

INK
Hold your horses, Nephew. This is how we are going to get you, to her.

ADAM
How? Do I put this thing on my back? What do I have to do?

INK
Wait. Let me feel this out. Oh yeah. Nephew, there's an old sacred ceremony we have to do before this thing can work.

ADAM
What is it? I'll do it!

INK
It was passed on to me by my grandfather, who got it from his father, by his father's father, by his father, and then by a lazy uncle. Now, I'm going to pass it on to you.

ADAM
Thank you, Uncle. I'm so honored. What do I have to do?

INK
Pull my finger.

ADAM
Will you stop playing around?

INK
Okay, all right, I'll stop. This is what you have to do, Nephew. Get in there.

ADAM
What?

INK
She looks at this thing every day for you. All you have to do is, is get in there, and I'll take you to her, and you and her can be together.

ADAM
Is this a trick?

INK
No. It'll be easy.

ADAM
You're not teasing me again?

INK
I'm not teasing you, Nephew. Just walk right into it.

ADAM
What if I break it?

INK
Well, I looked at it, and it didn't crack when I looked into it, so it should be safe for you.

ADAM
You couldn't find a set of wings?

INK
In this place I couldn't find a chicken bone. Now, go on.

[ADAM *approaches the circle. He watches* INK.]

ADAM
Don't push me.

INK
I won't, but just be careful of my foot that might follow you.

ADAM
What?

[*He crosses through the circle/mirror, and* INK *gives him a tap with his shoe.*]

INK
All aboard. Next stop—Snagville, *aye!* I've always wanted to say that.

ADAM
Uncle! Help me!

INK
Don't worry. You'll be all right. It's a little tight at first, but you'll get used to it.

ADAM
I don't know how long I can stay in here.

INK
It won't be long.

ADAM
You tricked me, Uncle!

INK
No. I'm helping you. Now be quiet, we're leaving now.

[INK *slowly shrinks the mirror/circle and exits.*]

Blackout. End of scene.

SCENE FOUR

Outside of THOMIE's *house.* THOMIE *is taking out the trash. She notices a figure standing near her dumpster.*

THOMIE
This will all go bad if I don't do this. I wish I still had my old dog Tulip. I—excuse me.

[INK *motions to her.*]

INK
Why hello there? I didn't mean to scare you. If you want me to, I can help you with that?

THOMIE
Who are you?

INK
You don't remember me? Good. I'm just a stranger.

THOMIE
Are you hungry?

INK
For a long time.

THOMIE
I was going to offer you some food, but if you're going to smart talk me . . .

INK
I'm sorry. I didn't mean to talk to you like that. It must be from this bump on my head.

THOMIE
I should go and get Shiyo. Bump? What bump?

INK
I got it when I was young.

THOMIE
Oh. You poor thing.

INK
Are you here by yourself?

THOMIE
No. And why do you ask?

INK
Just that a real good-looking woman like you couldn't possibly be here by herself. I thought someone might have "dated you out."

THOMIE
Yes, someone better than you.

INK
Ow.

THOMIE
Are you still hungry?

INK
Yeah. And my bump got bigger too.

[ADAM *from within the mirror.*]

ADAM
Uncle. Hurry up. I don't know how long I can stay here.

THOMIE
What did you say?

INK
It wasn't me. The bump, it must have been my bump.

THOMIE
I'll have my niece bring you something to eat, and a hat. Shiyo!

[INK *removes the small circle/mirror from his coat pocket and walks around the dumpster.*]

Bring some food out here, my girl. We have a strange, I mean, hungry man out here.

[ADAM *stands up.* SHIYO *enters with a plate of food.*]

This man, this, what is your name?

SHIYO
Adam? Adam!

THOMIE
Get away from us! Go on! Leave!

INK
Wait! They have to learn what happened. This is the only way it will end.

THOMIE
You take this—this thing—and get out of here.

INK
Please, they are both in trouble and this is the only way it will end.

[*A special on* SHIYO *and* ADAM.]

ADAM
I've . . .

SHIYO
Missed you, so long.

ADAM
So bad and the pain of not having you . . .

[*They hold each other.*]

SHIYO
You remember the night?

ADAM
We talk and tease each other.

SHIYO
You ask me to dance.

ADAM
It's a good drum.

[*We hear a couple's song. They dance.*]

SHIYO
It's a long song.

ADAM
Being with you makes it a good song.

SHIYO
You said you wanted to talk with me.

ADAM
Oh, yeah, uh, let's go to the top of the hill and so we can look down at the arbor, and see all the camps.

SHIYO
The sky is so clear and filled with stars.

INK

[*Calling.*]

You're not alone.

SHIYO
Of course not, I'm with Adam.

THOMIE
You are not alone.

ADAM
I was there, Shiyo, and no one else.

INK
Look around, again.

SHIYO
The sky is bright, and there are no clouds.

ADAM
Just a bright moon.

THOMIE
You are not alone.

SHIYO
Uh-huh. We were there, or here, by ourselves.

INK
No clouds, no dark rain clouds.

ADAM
We were here, I mean, we are here by ourselves.

THOMIE
You are not alone.

INK
Nephew, look over there. What do you see?

SHIYO
We were alone. There was no one else.

THOMIE
Who is that? Standing there?

ADAM
I said there was no one else!

THOMIE
You are not alone.

ADAM
There was no one else.

SHIYO
Wait. I see. Who is that?

INK
You are not alone.

ADAM
I don't know who that is? Wait. We are not alone . . .

SHIYO
What is he carrying? It looks like . . .

THOMIE
You are not alone.

INK
No clouds, no rain, no darkness, but a shadow.

SHIYO
Dinty? What do you want? Dinty? Speak up!

INK
A roar of thunder, or is it something else?

THOMIE
A flash of light, but no other flashes just this one?

[*A roar of thunder, a flash of light.*]

ADAM
I'm falling again.

SHIYO
No. I'll hold you.

ADAM
I'm falling Shiyo. Hang on to me.

SHIYO
I won't let you fall.

ADAM
I'm falling. I'll fall forever. Goodbye, my love, my girl.

SHIYO
No. Hang on to me, Adam. I don't want to let you go . . .

[*Special is out. Onstage we see* ADAM *lying on the ground.* SHIYO *is near him.* THOMIE *and* INK *stand near the two kids.*]

Adam. Please don't go. I can't hold you any—I love you. Adam.

INK
It's over. They can be on their ways. My beautiful wife, Thomie. Take your niece home.

THOMIE
And you my old man, Ink? What will you do?

INK
I'll take our nephew to his new home, out of this darkness, halfway, at least. I cannot go any further. I'll go back to nothingness. These two kids can now live in their worlds without feeling so bad, at rest and in peace. Oh, my wife, Thomie. My wife, I miss you. I wish to be standing with you in the world of you and my niece.

THOMIE
I miss you at nights and in the morning. I miss you in the day, at all times. What are you doing over there in that place? Are you falling too?

INK
No. I landed a long time ago.

Blackout. End of play.

Wink-Dah

Characters

TWO SHOE, human in appearance; around fifty years old; dressed in moccasins, pants, long sleeve shirt.

DEATH, wears a black hooded cloak in the first scene and carries a scythe. Later in the play he changes into an owl.

The Humans

JEREMY STONE, twenty years old.

VIRGIL STONE, younger brother to JEREMY. He is seventeen years old. He is wearing a pair of cheap, worn tennis shoes, a pair of faded jeans, a Levi's jacket, a T-shirt, and a headband.

ERNEST OLDROCK, friend to VIRGIL. He is fifteen years old. Dressed the same as VIRGIL, but with the exception of the headband.

VICTOR YOUNG, a farmer; he is fifty years old.

SCENE ONE

TWO SHOE *is sitting near a small fire warming his hands.*

TWO SHOE
Holy. Boy. I'm getting too young for this. I think. I've been on the road for a long time. I'm from up north there. Looking for a honey—*aye!* [*Laughs.*] Just kidding. You don't have to hold your honey that tight. Some people

call me Coyote, or Inkthomie. You can call me Two Shoe for now. I heard from my "Little Brother," Jeremy, there's a celebration going on. Today is camping day. Gives me a chance to have my dance leggings fixed.

[*Removes the leggings from a travel bag.*]

See? Just real pitiful, huh? [*Holds up the leggings.*] An extra sleeve? [*Smiles.*] Get all kinds of honies with that one. Anyway, I have a little brother, Jeremy. He said he'll make sure I have a place to stay at during the celebration. [*Pause.*] You see. A long time ago, I wanted a dancing outfit made for me. I went around and asked the women if they would make me one. "Err, no! Not for you, Two Shoe." I told them if they would they could be my honey. I guess they didn't want to risk it. I'm not a stink guy. But here— this one young woman walked up to me, she was really pretty, made my sleeve stiffen out. And she said in a real soft voice, "I'll make you a dancing outfit, Two Shoe." It wasn't even a woman. Made me jump out of bed. It was a young man. A *wink-dah*. And he made me the best dancing outfit around. [*Pause.*] That was a long time ago, and now, I need new leggings. Jeremy's my new "little brother." I only get to see him once a year at the celebrations. I saw him dancing one time and he looked real sad, lonesome. But I've got some good stories to tell him and some new songs to give him.

[*Two lights appear. They are headlights of a truck.*]

I suppose with everything changing this will change too. But I just hope it's for the . . . the

[*Truck stops. There are outlines of bodies. There is the sound of a door shutting.* DEATH *enters.*]

You shouldn't be driving like that. You might hit something—me! [*No response.*] You? Who are you?

[*No response.*]

What's your name?

[*No response.*]

Are you a stink guy, or what?

    [DEATH *crosses to* TWO SHOE.]

DEATH
I am the Grim Reaper.

TWO SHOE
Hem peepers? What about leggings? You do them too?

DEATH
The Grim Reaper.

TWO SHOE
Yeah? The way you look and drive, I bet. What do you do? Do you sing? Do you dance?

DEATH
When people die, I come to gather them. And then I take them to their destination. This last one was really heavy.

    [*Takes out a cigarette.*]

You got a light?

TWO SHOE
No. Oh . . . I can see who . . .

DEATH
Certainly not!

TWO SHOE
You must be what they call an angel?

DEATH
No. I'm . . .

TWO SHOE
A devil?

DEATH
Listen, you. I am Death. When people are ready to die I come to them.

TWO SHOE
Just people, huh? What about rocks, animals, and plants? You do them too?

DEATH
No. Of course not. Listen, you silly, whatever you are. I . . .

TWO SHOE
Ahhh . . . I know who you are! I know now. You are the *wah-ci-ju's* . . . I mean "white man's" death!

DEATH
Yes. Right. Are you sure you don't have a light . . . never mind.

[*He sits down near* TWO SHOE's *fire and lights his cigarette and enjoys the first puff.*]

Ahhh . . . nothing like a good smoke after a death. I suppose you don't have any manufactured pleasures? Walking? Boy, what a pleasure that is. Talking with animals, plants . . . So damn primitive.

TWO SHOE
Well at least I'll live . . . Oh. Excuse me.

[*Circles* DEATH.]

So, Death guy, what are you doing here?

DEATH
Cruising. A little detour before my next pick up.

[DEATH *raises his hand and snaps his fingers. The truck's engine stops.*]

TWO SHOE
Uh . . . Anybody I know?

DEATH
Maybe, maybe not. I was going to return home and change to make this next pick up. Damn humans. Give me a roadkill any day. They, these humans, want me to look like this, that, a spider, a snake, a goddamn owl, a raven, even a skeleton, until I gained five pounds, but the seasons are always hectic. I suppose I'll have to go as I am now.

TWO SHOE
Are you pickin' up an Indin, or a white guy?

DEATH
Well, if you must know . . . I . . . I'd better check.

[*Takes out a roll of paper from his cloak.*]

I did that one a day ago; I do hate trains, they were like plucking sardines from the can . . . And that plane crash, messy; I found them on top of a mountain, they were all over the place, here and there, luckily for me I had a rake and chains for the tires.

TWO SHOE
You have all the names written down of who's going to die and how?

DEATH
Yes.

TWO SHOE
Can I see?

DEATH
No.

[*Pause.*]

Maybe I should change now. I seem to have a little time, unlike some others.

TWO SHOE
What do you do, to change?

DEATH
A little of this and a lot of that.

TWO SHOE
I'll help you. I can hold your stuff for you.

DEATH
Save me a few steps back to the truck. Thank you. But the things you'll hold will be extremely heavy. Especially this.

[*Stands and holds out scythe.*]

TWO SHOE
No sweat.

DEATH
All right, here. And don't drop it. It's a new blade.

[*Drops the scythe into* TWO SHOE's *waiting hands.* TWO SHOE *nearly falls over.*]

And this.

[*He places the scroll into a small black bag and gives it to* TWO SHOE.]

You must not look inside of it. Do you promise me?

TWO SHOE
Sure.

DEATH
And don't interrupt me, or I won't be able to complete my change and continue my rounds. Now, excuse me for a bit.

[*He turns and* TWO SHOE *goes through the bag. When he opens it, there is a bright light. He finds the scroll.*]

TWO SHOE
Hey! No . . . That's nobody I know. December, February, June . . . Hey! Oh. I don't know him either. Oh no, there's Jeremy, "Little Brother." Hello

Jeremy. And who is that guy with you . . . He's . . . Some *wah-ci-ju*. And who's that other *wah-ci-ju*? What are they . . . No! No! Not there . . . It isn't a rightful way to leave . . . No! LOOK OUT JEREMY!

[DEATH *turns and is more of an owl in appearance. He grabs the scroll.*]

DEATH
What are you doing?

TWO SHOE
Nothing.

[*He slowly backs away from* DEATH *and drops the belongings of* DEATH.]

I'll see . . . I'll see you around, maybe not. Bye!

[*He starts to run, but* DEATH *reaches out and touches his shoulders, killing* TWO SHOE.]

DEATH
You can get up now.

Blackout. End of scene.

SCENE TWO

Jeremy enters. He goes inside of the teepee and hides underneath some blankets and sleeping bags. Inside of the teepee are two twin bed mattresses, cardboard boxes, a cooler, and a stove. Virgil enters carrying some boxes and a small suitcase. There is the sound of an owl.

Virgil enters the teepee. He sets the items down. Looks around to check the camping gear. He sees two feet sticking out from the pile of bedding. He picks up a hammer and a flashlight.

VIRGIL
Hey, I said hey!

[*No response.*]

You better get out of here!

[*No response. He uses the hammer to rap the feet.*]

JEREMY
OW!

VIRGIL
All right then!

[*Pulls the blankets and sleeping bags off of* JEREMY.]

JEREMY
Don't hit me! Please! Please don't hit me!

VIRGIL
Ho-lee, what happened to you?

JEREMY
Please . . .

VIRGIL
It's me, Virgil. Virgil! It's okay.

JEREMY
Don't hit me.

VIRGIL
I won't, but god, who did?

[*He tries to cover his head and hangs onto the blankets.*]

VIRGIL

[*Using the flashlight.*]

Ho-lee! What happened to you?

JEREMY
Please . . .

VIRGIL
It's me, Virgil. Virgil! It's okay.

JEREMY

[*Covering his eyes.*]

Don't hit me.

VIRGIL
I won't, but god, who did?

JEREMY
Christ! I'm not going to die. I suppose you wish I would.

VIRGIL
G'esus! That's . . . I got some aspirin. I think I have some.

JEREMY
You don't have to be doing this. . . .

VIRGIL
Are you sure?

JEREMY
It's none of your damn business anyway. Just finish putting up the camp. I'll redo it later.

VIRGIL
Shit. I didn't hear you at first is all! How was I to know it was you?

[*Begins to work and stops.*]

Fuck this. How did you get here?

JEREMY
I hitched . . . I walked . . . ran here.

VIRGIL
Jeremy? How did you lose your clothes? Jeremy?

JEREMY
Don't be asking me so much. I don't know.

VIRGIL
Are you . . . G'esus. You can tell me. Someone ought to know, hey.

[*No response.*]

I'll go and get Mom, she might be on her break now, and then I'll bring her out here.

[*He starts to leave.*]

JEREMY
Don't get Mom. Please. She'll just cry.

VIRGIL
You gonna tell me, hey?

JEREMY
If you listen, I will, but you have to listen hard.

VIRGIL
Yeah! I always have.

JEREMY
I still can't remember it all. I was with someone I really like . . . love . . .

VIRGIL

[*Softly to himself.*]

Shit.

JEREMY
And here—all I remember is this long song and drumbeats, all are loud and one right after the other. There's no break in between them. I was trying to

get between them, but I was pounded out. And then, there's this *wah-ci-ju*. Not even a song, he's yelling at me. I ran as fast as I can.

VIRGIL
Hey . . . Someone's after you? Shit! A white man?

[*No response.*]

Did he follow you here?

[*No response.*]

Jeremy?

JEREMY
I don't know! I don't think so.

VIRGIL
Goddamn you! Why the hell do you do things like this? Every time, Jeremy. It's celebration time and everyone will call you "Little Brother" . . . adopt you. And then have giveaways for you. People who don't know you will say, "He's so strong, this one called 'Little Brother' . . . Good he's that way—strong. But it's me. Me! I have to fight your battles for you. And I'm the youngest in our family. I'm the one who's strong. I should have the giveaways and the songs. These honors should be mine! Not you! Enit!

[*No response from* JEREMY.]

Shit! I'm the one, I'm the one who punches it out with older and bigger guys, both Indin and white. The old ones, the older people can stand you, but I, me, I fight the young ones who can't stand you. The ones who call you faggot and queer.

[*No response from* JEREMY.]

Damn. I hoped you would change. Everyone did.

ERNEST

[*Calling.*]

Virgil?

JEREMY
Who's that?

VIRGIL
Shhh . . .

ERNEST
Virgil? Hey! Stink guy!

VIRGIL
It's Ernest.

JEREMY
Don't answer him.

VIRGIL
Don't answer him?

ERNEST
Hey, Virgil. Honey, I'm home.

VIRGIL
Don't tell me what to do.

JEREMY
No! I don't want him in here!

VIRGIL

[*Goes to the teepee's entrance.*]

He won't talk.

[VIRGIL *goes out and waves to* ERNEST *and returns inside.* JEREMY *covers himself with blankets.*]

What the fuck are you supposed to be doing? G'esus.

ERNEST
Teepee prowling, Teepee creeping, teepee, teepee, pee-pee, hee-hee.

[ERNEST *enters.*]

ERNEST
Hello, Grandma?
Hey, Virgil, did you see him?

VIRGIL
Who?

[*No response.*]

ERNEST
You blind, or what? That white guy who drove into camp grounds? He stopped his truck near the arbor. He went into the weeds. Like Elmer Fudd on the rez. His truck is parked on the north end. Maybe somebody took his wife and is doing some real good poking with her.

VIRGIL
When was this?

ERNEST
I waited before I came here. Had to finish her off first.

VIRGIL
Bullshit. Which way did he head out?

ERNEST
He headed out, just like a baby, into the weeds. Walked right past your guy's camp. What were you doing? Doing nasty in the bedrolls. Better wash them before they get crusty.

VIRGIL
You should know. Don't be such a smartass. Did you do anything, Ernest?

ERNEST
Yeah. I was watching my auntie's tent.

VIRGIL
Real brave.

ERNEST
Fuck you, hey. I wasn't going to be that fucker's tourist guide. Maybe he's hunting gophers. You should go with him and clean them for him. Show him how it's done.

VIRGIL
Shit. Behave, hey.

[*Begins to work.*]

Ernest, do me a big favor?

ERNEST
What, grandma?

[*Laughs.*]

Burned you, huh? Just teasin' you. Don't be so serious, hey.

VIRGIL
Go outside and take a look around.

ERNEST
If I see that white guy?

VIRGIL
Who said anything about a white guy? Just come back here if you see him.

ERNEST
What if he follows me?

VIRGIL
Then you have a snag for the night. Christ. Go back to your auntie's tent, whatever's closer.

ERNEST
Yeah but—what if he's in my auntie's tent with a whole mess of dead gophers?

VIRGIL
Clean them and fry them up for him. And when you're done feeding him, give him a cup of tea, and visit with him. Christ, you sound like an old woman.

ERNEST
You. You go. Hey, Virgil, you go then. You're the one who's interested in this white guy. Getting all pissed off at me.

VIRGIL
Shit. All right, old woman. Don't dig around?

ERNEST
I won't.

[VIRGIL *gets a hammer and a flashlight.*]

Well?

[*No response from* VIRGIL.]

When you gonna go? Or are you frightened.

[*Scares* VIRGIL.]

Aye, like that one, huh?

VIRGIL
You shouldn't talk.

[*He exits.* ERNEST *watches.*]

ERNEST
Hurry! Run! Look at that stink guy run. Looks like a deer with hundred-pound antler. Oh, not too fast, Grandma, you'll have a blowout in your moccasins.

[*Goes digging into the boxes.*]

I wonder what Grandma brought her grandkids to eat. Maybe some Indin tube steak? Even some Spam. A mean Spam sandwich, with white gravy.

[*Finds the cooler.*]

T-bone bologna. The good kind. Uncle Oscar's special. Oh. Grandma really wants to camp.

[*Removes half a six-pack of beer.*]

Stink fucker guy wasn't going to share. Oh well, a mean sandwich. Indeed, my fellow council members. More Spam for the people.

[*He sits on the bedding.* JEREMY *groans.*]

JEREMY
Ohhh . . .

ERNEST

[*Jumps up.*]

Oh shit! Ghosts . . .

[*Steps back.*]

Oh.
It wasn't.

[*Laughs.* JEREMY *groans. He searches for a weapon and finds a skillet.*]

No wonder that stink guy left so quickly. Virgil. Virgil, is that you? Virgil. Because if not . . . Virgil . . . Virgil . . . Get back here. Virgil . . . Virgil. Ready or not, fucker . . . here it comes. What are you doing?

[*Raises the skillet.* VIRGIL *enters and stops* ERNEST.]

VIRGIL
What are you doing?

[ERNEST *drags* VIRGIL *closer to himself.*]

ERNEST
There's someone in here. You go first, over there.

[*Begins to exit.*]

I'll be right behind you.

VIRGIL
Behave. That guy's not around.

ERNEST
That's because he's in here with us.

VIRGIL
Will you settle down, G'esus! It's my brother.

ERNEST
Oh? Oh!

[*Sets skillet down.*]

You mean your sister.

[*Pulls back the blankets but it's the wrong end.*]

JEREMY
You little smartass shit.

ERNEST
Whoa! Who put the boots to you?

JEREMY
None of your damn business.

ERNEST
Well, I'm not hidden in the blankets like a girl.

JEREMY
You should have heard this one, big scare baby, "Virgil—Virgil—Vir . . ."

VIRGIL
Shut up! Both of you.

JEREMY
You tell him, not me.

VIRGIL
You want me to help you? Huh?

[*No response.*]

Good. Then you listen to me. There's a truck parked on the north side of here.

ERNEST
I wasn't shitting you, huh?

JEREMY
What are we going to do?

VIRGIL
I don't know? I didn't see him, though.

JEREMY
If we stay here, he might leave. We'll just have to be quiet and wait.

VIRGIL
Wait? G'esus. What for? To die? No.

JEREMY
What am I going to do?

ERNEST
What's he talking about, Virgil? Why's he all beat up?

JEREMY
Don't tell him. Stop looking at me, you little shit.

VIRGIL
Don't tell him? You haven't finished telling me.

ERNEST
Tell what? Hey? What?

VIRGIL
You'd better start.

ERNEST
Virgil?

VIRGIL
This white guy's looking for Jeremy, enit?

ERNEST
Him? Really? Ho-lee shit. What for?

JEREMY
You get me mad!

VIRGIL
I don't care! You'd . . . You'd better tell me what all happened.

JEREMY
Make him go first. He's all ears and a big mouth. This will be all over the rez by sun up. Stink, shit.

VIRGIL
Where's he going to go? I'm not going to send him out there with that white guy.

[*No response.*]

Now!

JEREMY
I feel all shamed out. I think . . . I think it's Victor, yeah, Victor Young.

VIRGIL
He's a farmer. A *wah-ci-ju*.

ERNEST
That's who this guy is? I knew I knew him.

VIRGIL
Hey! Settle down, Ernest!

[ERNEST *does*.]

What else?

JEREMY
All this time, I thought I knew it all. I thought I could get what I wanted and have it. The beginning of this summer, I went with Denise and those girls one night to the rodeo because they wanted me to come with them. I didn't want to. We were there for a couple of hours, and here, one of them wanted to meet this guy. They were drinking and then they started to give me a bad time. Showing off in front of those white cowboys.

ERNEST
Yeah. So?

JEREMY
So, let me finish.

ERNEST
So, hurry up. You're worse than listening to an old . . .

VIRGIL
Quiet!

JEREMY
I left them. I started walking back to town. I had on a pair of boots and my feet started to get tired. Then, then this pickup started to slow up behind me. I turned around to see who it was. I couldn't really see his face at first. I was waiting to hear, "Get off the road and back to your teepee, you blanket ass." It didn't come though. He asked me if I would buy for him. He offered me money, but I told him no. I got him a case of beer.

VIRGIL
Shhh . . . wait up.

ERNEST
What is it?

[*No response.*]

Virgil? Virgil?

VIRGIL
Nothing. I thought I heard something. Go ahead—talk.

JEREMY
Well, he asked me if I would drink with him. We drove up north of town and parked. I had some real good smoke, so I lit one up. It was his first time. He coughed and coughed. I slapped his back, it was like hitting a drum. We both laughed. It sounded good, this one and me. We started to see each other after that. Like two crows on a highway. Someone came by us, and we were gone. Around here, it has to be this way now. Tonight, I was bold. I went to his house for the first time. It was our first time. His father came in on us. We weren't doing anything wrong. His father didn't understand. He didn't know and wouldn't listen.

[*Pause.*]

The last few things, I remember. Someone hit me, and then I was hit again . . . I was lying on the floor. And someone was kicking me. Hard. I screamed. It stopped.

[*Pause.*]

Then there was this noise . . . loud and crunching. I think he broke my arm.

[*Holds up his arm.*]

I couldn't go home. I knew Mom would be setting up her camp. I am safe here. Our people are here.

VIRGIL
No. Oh no. Gary . . . Gary Young? Damn it!

[*Throws something at* JEREMY.]

ERNEST
Don't, Virgil!

VIRGIL
What the hell do you know?

ERNEST
He's your brother. I wouldn't be doing that to my brother.

VIRGIL
Shit. You? Ahhh . . .

[*Paces.*]

You think if we . . . we call the cops. You can be arrested for rape?

JEREMY
Yes . . . no . . . No! We didn't do anything wrong!

VIRGIL
What about Gary? Huh?

JEREMY
No. I can trust him. He wouldn't say anything like that.

ERNEST

[*Begins to leave.*]

Oh, well. I . . .

VIRGIL
Where you going?

ERNEST
It doesn't feel right, Virgil. I don't know if I want to hang around.

VIRGIL
Stay. I need your help, Ernest.

ERNEST
I don't know. Victor Young's out there with a gun, huh? What are we gonna do? Throw tent stakes at him?

VIRGIL
I've always helped you. I was the one who taught you to use a rifle and how to hunt. We'll protect Jeremy.

[*Turns to* JEREMY.]

We can do this. We can hide you until tomorrow. And in the morning, we can have one of Mom's friends, or one of your friends, have them take you back with them and keep you until this is over. We won't tell Mom. I can tell her later. Don't you leave this teepee, you here?

JEREMY
Yes, but what about Gary?

VIRGIL
To hell with him! He's not my blood. You, you're the one I have to protect. You're "Little Brother," not "Little-White-Brother."

ERNEST
Should we start sharpening tent stakes, or what?

VIRGIL
I got rifles.

ERNEST
Yeah. Who's gonna get them?

VIRGIL
You.

ERNEST
Oh shit. I should'a stayed home tonight. There aren't any girls out here tonight anyway.

VIRGIL
Come on. After this is over, I bet you'll get an eagle feather. Maybe even a song. Then you'll have all kinds of girls chasing you down.

ERNEST
Really? Okay, I guess. How am I going to get to your house?

VIRGIL
Take my car.

JEREMY
Less people around the camp. He should just stay here with us.

VIRGIL
Quiet! You don't have say in this. Only I do.

[*Turns to* ERNEST.]

Don't worry. I thought of that too, but I don't think he'll do anything.

ERNEST
Then how come you don't go and get the rifles. Why should we anyway?

VIRGIL
If he sees me, he'll guess where Jeremy's at. It would be easy to pull my car off the road between here and town. You should go, Ernest. He's never seen you before. Better safe than sorry, too.

ERNEST
For you, all right. I guess. What do you all want me to do?

VIRGIL
Go and get my rifles. The shells will be in my top drawer. Oh yeah. There's an envelope there too. Bring it.

ERNEST
And? Should Grandson bring anything else from the store?

[*No response.*]

Guess not. Let me have your keys.

[*He gets the keys and exits.*]

VIRGIL
Good. He's a man. Grandpa and Grandma said boys grow up to be men, and men are warriors, not *wink-dahs*.

JEREMY
I'm something, too. I belong here, too. You're not the only one of this circle.

VIRGIL
This is the last time, Jeremy. You hear?

JEREMY
Yes. But you better hear me.

[VIRGIL *begins to exit.*]

VIRGIL
I'll be back.

JEREMY
Where are you going? Stay with me. You're supposed to protect me. What about Victor Young?

VIRGIL
I'm going to look around. I want to know where he's at. I hope he's strong and not weak.

JEREMY
No. Don't leave me Virgil? Virgil?

Blackout. End of scene.

SCENE THREE

TWO SHOE *lies on the ground.*

TWO SHOE
Oh . . .

[*Stands up.*]

What . . . Hey! Is that me?

[*Points to an outline of his body resting on the ground. It is the shadow of* TWO SHOE.]

DEATH
Yes. You kind of remind me of a gopher on the highway all spread out like that.

TWO SHOE
What happened to me? You didn't . . .

DEATH
Why don't you join me?

TWO SHOE
How could you do that to me? You didn't even give me a chance to get ready. I . . . I'm a ghost, huh?

DEATH
It's not a big deal, you know.

TWO SHOE
I was doing pretty good in the other world. Everything was good because I had a direction, and now, I don't know what path I'm supposed to follow. I wasn't cockeyed. . . . You've made everything cockeyed for me. Why me?

DEATH
I told you not to look at the list. "Don't look at the list," I asked you, but no, you being nosey, you had to look. Right in the middle of my change. A million dead people with no place to go, just because of you.

TWO SHOE
It wasn't that bad. Nothing could be that bad.

DEATH
Not bad, huh? You were teasing me. You called me a stink guy. I am not stink.

TWO SHOE
I remember now, stink guy. *Aye*, don't get mad.

[*Feels himself.*]

Ewww . . . Almost made me cry . . . No gunshot wound, no rope, no knife, not even inside myself did I feel there was something wrong. Wet myself. Just stiffened out and fell.

[*Thinks for a moment.*]

But hey! How come I didn't see my name on the list. Let me check.

DEATH

[*He does.*]

Uh. What was your name?

TWO SHOE
Shame me out. Forgotten already. Two Shoe!

DEATH
Two Shoe, Two Show, Two Hands, Two Hawks, Two Hats Blue, just teasing . . . Nope!

TWO SHOE
You didn't kill for the fun of it, huh?

DEATH
Well, no, uh, I killed you but it wasn't. I . . .

TWO SHOE
I don't like being dead, hey. I didn't have a chance to let anyone know. No funeral, no wake, not even a feast. And now that I'm here you haven't even given me a direction to go.

[*Walks away from* DEATH.]

You're no fun hey!

[*Thinks a moment.*]

I'll accept death and even though you claimed me in your white man's form. If you do one thing.

DEATH
No, no, no deals. Absolutely not. There is no way I can and will change anything for any purpose, or anyone. And . . .

TWO SHOE
How about if we play a little game?

DEATH
Game? What kind of game? No, no, I can't . . .

TWO SHOE
We could set down some stakes. Like if I win . . .

DEATH
You win what?

TWO SHOE
You bring me back into the other world.

[JEREMY *has dressed and is searching in one of the suitcases.* VIRGIL *sits near the teepee's entrance and is drinking.*]

JEREMY
I had it in my suitcase. You didn't take it out, did you?

[*No response.*]

You know. You could pray. It would help you now, more than that shit will. I'll help you if you want me too. You remember how Grandpa showed us.

[*Laughs.*]

Better'n any priest.

[VIRGIL *is drinking.*]

VIRGIL
I'll be ready. Don't you worry.

JEREMY
Found it.

[*Removes his medicine bundle from the suitcase.*]

I'll never take it off. My friend helped me with this. You should have one, too. It could help you now.

VIRGIL
What's a *wink-dah* doing with a medicine bundle? I don't need it. You'll need everything you can get your hands on. Not me.

JEREMY
You're talking drunk. Trying to be big. What do you see? How do you see things, Virgil? Everything must be all crooked in your eyes. Just all . . . crooked.

VIRGIL
But I'm strong, not weak, like you.

[ERNEST *enters carrying the rifles.*]

ERNEST
It was easy, cheesy. Like that, huh? Two rifles and a box of shells for each rifle.

VIRGIL
Good going, Ernest. Where are the shells?

[*Takes the rifles.*]

ERNEST
Here . . . Pigged out on the beer, huh?

VIRGIL
Christ! These aren't the right ones.

ERNEST
Oh. Don't get mad, Grandma. Grandson wouldn't let you down.

[*Gives him another box of shells.*]

DEATH
Okay, okay, I can do that, no problem.

TWO SHOE
And you allow my "Little Brother"—Jeremy, to die in a peaceful death. By the path of his people, the generations, not cockeyed like I am.

DEATH
And if you lose, Two Shoe?

TWO SHOE
If, if, you can keep me. I'll live in this unbalanced way. And since I have to do that, you then have to spare the life of Jeremy, "Little Brother."

DEATH
We're not asking for much, are we? Let me think this one over a little.

[*Paces.*]

What do you want to play?

TWO SHOE
Oh, I don't know? Let me think . . . What do you want to play?

[DEATH *and* TWO SHOE *race for their bags.*]

DEATH
Ummm . . . Chess?

[*Takes out a board and* TWO SHOE *shakes his head.* DEATH *does a simple hand trick and produces a deck of cards.*]

Five-card draw—deuces are wild? Baseball?

TWO SHOE
Nah.

[DEATH *pulls board back out again.*]

DEATH
Checkers?

[*No response.*]

Uhhh, Par-cheez-zie!

TWO SHOE
You're not even close.

DEATH
Trivial Pursuit?

TWO SHOE
Don't you know anything good?

DEATH
All right. You suggest a game we can play, if you know so much.

TWO SHOE
All right. What about a . . . a . . . stick game?

[*Goes through his bag.*]

DEATH
Nah! Don't go ethnic on me, I haven't changed yet.

TWO SHOE
Oh. All right. How about horse racing?

DEATH
Nope.

TWO SHOE
Since you haven't fully changed from your white man's death to my people's death. You do kinda look like an owl. Anyways, why don't we play this game? A shell game?

DEATH
Where are we going to get shells?

TWO SHOE
We could use my ears.

DEATH
Where are we going to get a third ear?

TWO SHOE
How about getting it off one of your bodies? And we'll use a pebble, sound good to you?

DEATH
Yeah, I guess. Let's find one.

TWO SHOE
Wait. I'll find us one. You go and get your ear. The pebble we use has to be special.

[*Searches for a pebble.* DEATH *goes to get the ear.*]

Brothers, Brothers, Sisters, Sisters, Cousins, Friends, all my relations, help me and Jeremy. Help us.

[*Picks up a pebble.*]

Will you help me and Jeremy? You will? Good. Then when you are underneath my ear, whisper. And I'll find you.

[*Listens to the pebble.*]

Okay. I found one.

[DEATH *returns with an ear.*]

DEATH
Great. This one was hard of hearing. Let's play. You can do the picking. If you find the pebble three out of five, you win. If you don't, too bad. Let me give you a warning, Two Shoe. Nothing moves faster or strikes as silently as me.

[*They begin the game.*]

Okay. Which ear?

TWO SHOE
What?

DEATH
WHICH EAR!

TWO SHOE
You don't have to yell. I'm not deaf, I just don't have any ears. Just wait . . . What?

DEATH
What?

TWO SHOE
This one.

DEATH
You're right. You win one. Okay. Again.

[*Lifts the ear. Mixes the ears.*]

Pick, pick, pick, pick.

TWO SHOE
Don't go so fast.

DEATH
I'm not. Pick, pick, pick, pick . . . Which one? Huh?

TWO SHOE
Oh, uh . . . that one.

DEATH

[*Lifts the ear.*]

Whoaaa . . . Wait a minute here.

TWO SHOE
What's wrong?

DEATH
I wasn't born yesterday, you know.

TWO SHOE
What do you mean?

DEATH
Have you said anything to that pebble?

TWO SHOE
No. It can't talk, or hear.

DEATH
How do you know that?

TWO SHOE
That's what it said when I asked it.

DEATH
Oh. Well then . . . Wait a minute.

TWO SHOE
No, don't pout. Do you want a chance to pick?

DEATH
Yes.

TWO SHOE
Here we go then.

[*Mixes the ears.*]

All right.

DEATH
That one.

TWO SHOE
That was kind of fast. Are you sure?

[DEATH *nods, "yes." He lifts the ear.*]

What do you know! Again?

DEATH
Yes. Of course.

[*Game starts again.*]

That one.

TWO SHOE
My fingertips haven't even touched air yet from leaving the ears and you're ready to pick?

DEATH
Yes. That one.

[TWO SHOE *lifts the ear.*]

TWO SHOE
You are quick and silent, huh?

Blackout. End of scene.

SCENE FOUR

JEREMY
You shouldn't be saying any of those things Virgil. You shouldn't be making fun of it.

VIRGIL
What's in there? What did you and your little friends gather for your medicine? A few daisies, a mirror, and a brush?

JEREMY
No! You're just talking stupid. It was my brother, Two Shoe. He helped me find the things I need.

VIRGIL
Well, let me see it?

JEREMY
You know I can't do that. Maybe one of these days you'll have one.

VIRGIL
But it'll be for a warrior, not a *wink-dah*.

JEREMY
You shit.

VIRGIL
You listen to me! Remember? I'll get us out of this. Just like the other times. And after this is over, you'll owe me. All right? You'll owe me.

JEREMY
What? What do you want?

VIRGIL
This shit is going to stop. I'll say it does, not you. You'll have to change. You can't be *wink-dah*.

ERNEST
Pretty damn good, huh? When I was going I was thinking about how I would sneak these babies in. Just like mission impossible, enit? One thing

though, Virgil. I couldn't find that envelope you told me about. I looked all over in your drawer. And I couldn't find the sucker.

VIRGIL
What took you so fucking long?

ERNEST
Don't fucking talk like that to me, hey! What was in the envelope, hey! Pay-gee?

VIRGIL
No! An eagle feather. My grandpa gave it to me. He gave it to me after I killed my first buck. I'm a warrior.

JEREMY
Huh-uh! It's to protect you. You can't . . .

VIRGIL
Shut up!

   [*Turns to* ERNEST.]

You, Ernest. Take this rifle and walk around the outside of the camp grounds. You see Victor Young, get him.

ERNEST
That's real easy, Grandma. Just like in the olden days, huh? Scare his white farmer's ass off our land. Just shoot and watch him run.

VIRGIL
Shit. Shoot at him? No. Kill him.

ERNEST
You want to kill him? Virgil, it's not like we're hunting this guy and gonna scare him away. You want to kill him. They'll get me for murder. No. You kill him if you want to. I can't.

VIRGIL
Okay, fucker! You won't help your brother defend his family. Let that get around the rez. Let them know you're a coward. Maybe you're *wink-dah* yourself!

ERNEST
Fuck you, hey! I don't want to kill!

VIRGIL
I thought I could count on you. You should go. You don't mean anything to me.

[*Turns his back on* ERNEST.]

ERNEST
Don't do this to me, Virgil. Please don't turn your back on me.

[*No response.*]

JEREMY
Virgil!

ERNEST
Virgil?

JEREMY
This is your friend. What's making you do this?

[*No response.*]

What's making you do this?

[*No response.*]

Listen to me! You said you would not do this to him. You claim to be his brother. How can you treat him this way?

VIRGIL

[*Turns to face* ERNEST.]

You. You're afraid to fight, huh? And you're telling me how I should act? But I lead here, huh? You both need me, so both of you should do as I say.

JEREMY
Yes.

VIRGIL

[*To* ERNEST.]

You don't have to do it, Ernest. I'll kill him, but if Victor Young turns around and starts shooting at you, I sure the hell hope you have the guts to shoot back at him.

JEREMY
It's just the beer talkin', Ernest.

VIRGIL
Yes, he will! He won't see any difference. Just like in the olden days, one Indin is the same.

ERNEST
I don't want to die.

VIRGIL
Then don't be so scared about having to fight back.

ERNEST
I'm not . . . I just . . .

[*Looks at the rifle.*]

You'll, you'll be out there with me, Virgil?

VIRGIL
Yeah, yeah. Go to the south entrance and work your way all the way around the grounds, in a circle. You see Victor Young, make a sound, an owl, or something. I'll be there as fast as I can. You do the same for me. Now take the rifle.

ERNEST
All right.

[*Paces.*]

There'll be three of us, huh? You'll be out there for me?

[VIRGIL *nods, "yes."*]

All right then.

[*He exits.*]

JEREMY
You shouldn't have done that to him. I suppose, two warriors. Two *pitiful* warriors is more like it. Call him back in here. What if he gets shot, Virgil? Then what? He winds up dead because of you. No. He didn't have to go. This has been nothing but bullshit! I'm going to call him back. What is he going to do? . . .

VIRGIL
What's he going to do? He'll fight. Shit! People accuse me of being like you. Not because of what I did, but because we are of the same blood. And here—I am the only one who will stick up for you.

[*Loads the other rifle.*]

You're the only one of your kind around here. Maybe if things change . . . it will be okay for you to be *wink-dah*. But not now. You should really think about changing what you are. It would be a lot easier for mom and me.

JEREMY
You ask a lot of me, little . . . youngest brother.

[*No response.*]

Remember Grandma Rose? She knew what I am. She loved us both because we are of the same blood, but we weren't the same, in what we are in life.

[*No response.*]

She was the one who taught me how to sew. Taught me a song to sing.

[*Works on a pair of dance leggings.*]

After this is over. I'll stay with my own kind. I'll go to different celebrations off the rez. I'll be humble. I won't cross over to the white man's world again. This is our world and I'll stay here. It won't ever happen again. Look. Look.

[*Holds up the leggings.*]

I finished these. I started them a few days ago. I found them in your dancing outfit case. You can wear them tomorrow night. You'll be the first one of your group when they have grand entry.

[*No response.*]

Look Virgil. These leggings are blue. For Whirlwind Soldier.

[*No response.*]

Look. My arm isn't broken. Feel it. It's just bruised is all. And here I was really complaining about how bad it is.

[*No response.*]

Virgil?

[*No response.*]

The cops will be here soon anyways. They always check the grounds on camping day. That's the reason why I didn't want you to be mad at Ernest. This is our teepee, everyone knows it. It's our circle. And when Gary comes . . . we'll both be protected . . . safe. You and Ernest will be out there playing Dirty Harry. I know non-Indins aren't a part of your world, but Gary is a part of my world.

VIRGIL
"Because Gary's a part of my world." Shit. Do you really believe that? Then why the hell isn't he here? You are right about one thing, this white man is a part of your world, not mine! Every time I tried to make the non-Indin a part of mine, it's made a cut in me. We're going to live in peace.

Mom and Dad used to believe that too. Dad's gone now, and Mom doesn't think that way anymore. And no matter where you are, Oil Celebration, Frog Creek Celebration, or what you do, it's always turned out bad for us because you're a *wink-dah*.

[*No response.*]

Grandma Rose used to tell me how things are going away, you never see them again, like the buffalo, chiefs, even sundances at one time, you never see them again. And now, you should go away like the other things Grandma was telling me about.

[*No response.*]

You know something, Jeremy. I've never wanted to say this. But now, for you, I will. You shame me out. You shame me all inside of myself. I have nothing but shame. Every time and everything you've done has caused me a new cut of shame. And if you don't change, I will disown you as my brother.

JEREMY
You're lying! Don't say that to me! The buffalo have come back, and the chiefs have returned. The sundance is alive, but the difference is between these things and me is that I am your brother, for today, tomorrow, always. I am of your blood.

[*No response.*]

I am *wink-dah*. I sing songs people have forgotten, and the song lives again. I help people pass peacefully from this world into the other world. I take their cockeyed vision and make it straight. And this isn't new, Virgil. It's old, older than Grandma Rose. And I am good to my people, our people. Gary too. And I would never do anything bad to them.

[*No response.*]

Virgil, if I could heal your shame, just like any other wound, I would. I can try. Please. I suppose it's not too late, huh? Let me try, brother; at least let me try?

VIRGIL
Grandma said that sometimes there are wounds that won't heal.

[*No response.*]

You want to try, huh? But do you trust me?

JEREMY
Of course, I do.

[*Watches* VIRGIL.]

I suppose . . . ! I have nothing else in this world, but my family, you.

VIRGIL
You'll do anything I say?

JEREMY
Yeah. What do you . . . ?

VIRGIL
Good, because I want you to do something for me. Show me you trust me.

JEREMY
It's a start, huh, brother?

VIRGIL
Yeah. I want you to tie your leg with the anchor rope.

JEREMY
What? Are you losing your mind?

VIRGIL
If you're so good, and now you have power, the medicine given to you by your friend, I want you to tie your leg up with the anchor rope.

JEREMY
Are you mad? Don't even think it, brother.

VIRGIL
Do it!

[VIRGIL *gets the rope and offers it to Jeremy.*]

JEREMY
Will you sober up and hear yourself. You've been watching to many damn mov . . . You do it then!

[VIRGIL *does.*]

See.

[*Pulls on the rope.*]

See! I will be all right, Virgil, my brother.

VIRGIL
It's not over yet.

[*Goes to one of the boxes and gets a knife.*]

Your medicine won't help us. Here.

[*Offers the knife.*]

Here!

[*Places the knife in* JEREMY's *hand.*]

If you get scared, cut yourself free. I'll kill this white man, and then you'll owe me my life back.

JEREMY
You take it! I am strong. I don't owe you anything.

[*Gives the knife back to* VIRGIL.]

I haven't done anything wrong. It's this world, not me.

VIRGIL
I'll be outside. Don't be scared.

[*Exits.*]

JEREMY
Don't you be scared. You talk more like a killer than a warrior.

[*He hops over to the mattress and sits. He picks up a pair of leggings and begins to sew. We hear an owl.*]

If Gary were here, he would show you what a warrior is. Never thought about that, did you? Gary . . . Gary, when you start hunting this fall you can get all kinds of deer. And then I'll make the deer hides into white buckskin, real soft. I know how to prepare it. I'll do it. My mother taught me how to. My mom used to pray before she skinned the deer. She used to hang it up from the back of its legs on the clothesline. In the fall, when she pulls back the deer hide from the meat, you can see the steam rise. She never hurried and never wasted the meat or damaged the hide.

[*Pause.*]

You're gonna have to get a lot of deer, Gary. I'll make you a dance outfit of white buckskin. You and me. We'll travel to different celebrations. I have a lot of relatives. So, we can go all over. Even to Canada.

[*Sound of an owl.*]

We could live someplace else. We could go now.

[*He starts to gather his sewing and begins to pack a suitcase.*]

Let's go. Just you and me. I'll get you. And we can live and not have to worry about what people think about us. We won't be afraid. Like now

[*A knife tears into the side of the teepee.* VICTOR YOUNG *enters with a rifle.*]

VICTOR
You stay right where you are.

JEREMY
Gary? No . . . No . . .

[*He tries to go for the door, but* VICTOR *hits him with the rifle.*]

VICTOR
Shut up! Shut up . . .

JEREMY
Gary? Where is he?

VICTOR
Shut up! Don't you ever say my son's name to me again, you sick bastard. Never again.

[JEREMY *tries to crawl away from* VICTOR *but he is tied and goes into a circle.*]

JEREMY
Gary. Help me! Please help me, Gary.

VICTOR
Stop it! Don't use his name.

[*Strikes* JEREMY.]

Do you hear me? Don't say his name.

JEREMY
No!

VICTOR
Do you hear me! You . . . you raped my son . . . Like some goddamn animal; you waited until I was gone, and then you broke into my house and raped my son. Didn't you?

JEREMY
No! That isn't true.

VICTOR
I know it is.

JEREMY
Bring Gary here! Bring him here, I want to see him. He'll tell you to your face.

VICTOR
No! Our blood is good. We didn't raise him like you . . . He couldn't be like you.

JEREMY
Bring Gary here!

VICTOR
No! Shut up!

JEREMY
What have you done to Gary?

VICTOR
Stop saying my son's name, you son of a bitch!

[*Points the rifle barrel at* JEREMY's *face.*]

We tracked you all the way here. I've given you more of a chance than you gave my son.

JEREMY
Go ahead. I'm here in my circle. Gary will join me here within it. You warriors want to rule this world. But in my world, Gary and I will be together. Shoot me.

[JEREMY *grabs the rifle.* VICTOR *tries to break free.*]

VICTOR
No! Gary! My son—we are strong . . . We . . . We tracked this big four-point buck all the way to the slough. We didn't give up. It's headed there,

and I'll be damned, it is. Just like I said. My aim is still sharp. Didn't bat an eyelash, I squeezed off a shot. He fell.

[*Pause.*]

Ass over tea kettle. Ran so damn fast over to it, ready to pack it out. The deer was still alive. They do that sometimes. And it moved its head and cut his hand. Damn antlers. Cut was wide open. I came running over. Screaming so loud, me and Gary, I didn't know who was the loudest.

[*Pause.*]

Christ, I was scared. I thought he was hurt real bad. He was holding his hand tight to himself. I had to pry his hand away from his body. He didn't want to show me because he's ashamed. He's scared he'll let me down. All I want him to do is learn about life. Nobody can ask for more. I pried his hand free to see the cut. It was pretty deep. 1 used part of my shirt to wipe away the blood. It's pretty damn deep.

[*Pause.*]

Tonight . . . I . . . I . . . I took his hand and put it to my chest. I could feel the warmth of his blood. It soaked through my shirt. I couldn't wipe the blood away. I tried to hold onto his hand, but it was busted up . . . I held his head near my chest. I could feel the warmth of his blood, but I couldn't feel the warmth of his body. And then his body started to shake. I held on to him as tight as I could. Trying to stop him from shaking. That's why he's losing his warmth. But . . . when he stopped shaking . . . he went and left . . . his old man. . . .

JEREMY
You . . . You killed Gary?

[*Thinks a moment.*]

No! No!

VICTOR
Gary, I'm sorry. Please help me . . .

JEREMY
Has this whole world gone cockeyed?
I got him!
Ernest! Ernest! I got him!

VICTOR

> [*Reaching for* JEREMY.]

Will you help me?

> [*A gun shot.* VICTOR *falls backward.*]

VIRGIL

> [*Enters.*]

I got him!

> [*Calling back out of the teepee.*]

I got him!

> [*To* JEREMY *who is crying over* VICTOR's *body.*]

No! Not for him! Don't you cry for him. You cry for me, your family, not for him. He was going to kill you.

JEREMY
What?

> [*Grabs* VIRGIL.]

No! I'm still alive. You killed him!

VIRGIL
You listen to me, Jeremy! You'd better listen, hey! He was going to kill you. That's what you'll tell people when they ask you. That's what you tell in the songs you sing about this. Do you hear me!

JEREMY
I hear . . .

VIRGIL

[*Calling.*]

Ernest! *Eh-he-hey!*

[*To* JEREMY.]

Remember, *wink-dah.*

[ERNEST *enters.*]

ERNEST
What happened? I heard . . . is that him?

VIRGIL
I got him! First coup! Just in time too. He was ready to kill Jeremy, enit? Enit, Jeremy?

JEREMY
Yes . . .

ERNEST
Is he dead?

[VIRGIL *sets his rifle down and kneels down to the body and rolls it over.*]

You're fucking crazy, hey!

VIRGIL
See. Ernest!

[ERNEST *becomes sick and looks for a place to run. He crawls underneath the teepee's covering and exits.*]

ERNEST
No! No fucking way!

VIRGIL
Ernest! Ernest! Get back here!

[*Turns to* JEREMY.]

Ernest doesn't know I had to do this. I couldn't have done anything else. I had to do it, or you would've been killed.

[*No response.*]

You owe me.

JEREMY
What?

VIRGIL
Jeremy!

[*No response.*]

Do you hear me?

JEREMY
Yes.

VIRGIL
You have to change. You can't be *wink-dah*. Not until I say it's okay. And . . . And only when I say it's okay.

JEREMY
Virgil. Let's take him to the hospital? He still might be alive. I'll tell the cops I did it. Okay? Huh? We'll use your car. Don't be afraid. I'll face the FBI.

[JEREMY *tries to move* VICTOR.]

He wasn't going to kill me! You are!

VIRGIL
You're talking crazy.

JEREMY
Is this going to heal you? Huh? This is it? You think this will take away the shame? I suppose, you never knew what it is to feel shame inside. I do.

VIRGIL
Shut up!

[*Hits* JEREMY.]

I'm going to track down that fuckin' Ernest and bring him back here. You stay here. You hear me? And then when I get back, I'll decide to call the cops. You better be here when I get back! You hear me?

JEREMY
Yes.

[VIRGIL *exits.*]

VIRGIL

[*Calling.*]

Ernest! Ernest!

JEREMY
Damn you! Damn you, Virgil.

[*Pause.*]

And now what am I going to do? How am I supposed to live in this world of white men and warriors?

[*Crawls to* VICTOR.]

How are you going to find Gary? You're leaving this world in a violent way. How do you know you will reach Gary? I'll help you. You can reach the other world. I know a way. You can find Gary. Both of you don't have a song to leave this world. You can have mine.

[*Sings a song for* VICTOR. *He takes a blanket and covers* VICTOR. *Then he crawls over to the anchor rope. He begins to build a small mound using the blankets, sleeping bags, and boxes. He gets up on top of the mound. Then he unties the anchor rope from the anchor stake and makes a loop in the rope and places his feet into the loop. Then he pulls on the rope and tightens the loop and lifts his legs into the air and into the loop. He takes a kitchen knife.*]

Grandfathers, I cannot live in this world. Forgive me, I can't live being not what you made me. Please forgive my brother. Heal his heart. Make him strong. Don't let him go insane. Please help these other two people find the world they go to. I thank you for making me what I am. I'm sorry I have failed you.

[*He hangs upside down from the rope.*]

When Grandpa killed a deer. He would cut the throat of the deer, so the blood would go back to the mother earth. And that way, the mother would have something to drink, something to eat, and she would never thirst again.

[*He slits his throat and hangs from the rope.*]

Blackout. End of scene.

EPILOGUE

DEATH *enters the teepee. He looks around.* TWO SHOE *enters. He is running and stops outside of the teepee.* VIRGIL *is covered in mud and sits with his knees underneath himself.* VIRGIL *raises his head and then drops it.* TWO SHOE *enters the teepee.*

TWO SHOE
Jeremy . . . Little Brother . . .

[*He goes to* JEREMY *and lowers* JEREMY. *He finds a blanket and covers him.* TWO SHOE *finds the pair of leggings and places them on* JEREMY's *body.* DEATH *walks over and places the medicine bundle around* JEREMY's *neck.*]

DEATH
You couldn't trick me. You couldn't stop me.

TWO SHOE
No. I couldn't. But why here? Why this place? Like this?

DEATH
I know no boundaries, race, religion. I come, and I leave with someone. But this is the first time anyone really cared for another person. You for Little Brother—he for these two *wah-ci-jus*. Things have changed, Two Shoe.

TWO SHOE
There are many things that have changed in this world. And it needs so many things. It needs him. Couldn't you have left my . . . "Little Brother"? Of all the visions in this world, he had kept to his own. He didn't go cockeyed like the rest of us. We'll never know what it's like to see straight, enit?

Blackout. End of play.

To Cross

Characters

RAVE, a young man in his late teens
BIRD, an elderly man, timeless

Setting

Place: At the edge of a dry riverbank
Time: 1970s

RAVE *holds an old canvas duffle bag.*

RAVE
Right over there. That's where some of them went. Across the way there. Between those willows and past the cottonwoods.

   [*Points with his lips.*]

Do you know if any of them came back?

BIRD
Yeah. Some them came back, and they were different, in the clothes they were wearing, or the shoes and coats they had on, but age will do that to a person. Except your cousin Amy.

RAVE
Some say she was never the same. She would never talk to anybody, or would talk with anybody.

BIRD
She was that way because she was never really raised with us. Her parents kept here away from the people. As she grew older she wanted it that way too. Amy did come and visit, but it was like she was reminding herself she lives better. She didn't want to be one of us until late in her life. She followed that guy, can't remember his name, but he was leading all those who crossed and were trying to cross back again. He didn't know anything, and he wasn't from here.

RAVE
Will I think differently?

BIRD
No, but if you are lucky, you will be able to think more. See things we don't, know things we will only talk about from rumors, stories, and even dreams. Your thoughts might be large, but your heart will keep them grounded.

RAVE
Do I have to go over there? Do I have to leave? Why can't I stay? I like it here.

BIRD
You've always talked about crossing over to that side. Now's your chance. Go over there and see what's there. They have all kinds of things over there. When they started building on this land they brought all kinds of things from all parts of the world. The world came here, and if you cross you can go see. You can come back and tell me.

RAVE
Come with me then?

BIRD
I can't. This is your time now, not mine. I had my chance a long time ago. When I was over there, they had places I couldn't go because I was an Indian. Those things are gone, so I've heard, so you will see more.

RAVE
What if I don't come back? What if I get lost, and I can't find my way back?

BIRD
That's a very crazy thought? What's going to happen? Are you going to get hit in the head and forget everything? No. Just get yourself ready and go. If you want to stay, then stay but remember that we'll be here.

RAVE
Will people be mad at me for going? I remember how they told some who went over that when they came back they had turned white—or acted white.

BIRD
Well, some of them are part white. They behaved that way here, and when they crossed over to there, they felt right at home. Some of them were so resentful about having to come back. Some became so afraid they would come back and never cross again. Some of the people who crossed were so resentful of being a part of us they killed us over and over again in their minds. Are you afraid of this?

RAVE
No. At least, I don't think I am.

BIRD
You've never said or done anything to show me you are that way.

RAVE
Then how come those others turned that way?

BIRD
Don't know. In these newer generations things change. Evolve is what some say.

RAVE
I thought you knew all the answers. You've crossed a lot in your life.

BIRD
Over there, they are the same to me as they are here. I can't tell the difference. I get it from both sides. It doesn't bother me. I have no stake with either side. You, you have something on both sides. You'll have to cross over. And you can always come back. Unless you die.

RAVE
Thanks.

BIRD
Hey, Rave, but even if you do die, they'll ask for your body to be returned. I know they will. Me, they'll stick me in a cardboard box or in a garbage can.

RAVE
I have to find more human friends.

BIRD
That's what they are, on both sides. So, get your things and just walk over there. From one world to another. Just go on over there. Your generations can have two worlds. Make the best of it.

RAVE
You'll come with me?

BIRD
I'll be here and over there. I'm always the same.

RAVE
I hope that happens to me.

BIRD
Rave, you'll know both my names. They'll have two different meanings, but just one person.

RAVE
Me too? Having two names?

BIRD
Maybe, one might die over there, while the other part lives over here. Or this part over here might die, and the part over there will live? So hard to say what will happen to memories and dreams. A part of you might die, or a part of you will always be the same. Never changing. They'll look at you over there as they see you over here. You will always be an Indin. That you have to keep yourself. Give it to no one or any agent.

RAVE
You know, Bird, things have changed so much. There really isn't that big of a difference today from there and here. We watch it all the time, hear it in different stories, all that information about over there is here.

BIRD
Do you really kick in on all that information? Or are you like some of your friends who just glaze over it? Don't think it means you or touches you?

RAVE
I think about what's over there. What might happen to me over there?

BIRD
Does it change the way you think here, Rave? If something falls over there, do you walk around here and push something over? You know, to keep things in order?

RAVE
No. I don't have to, not always. You know what, Bird? I'm not afraid of going over there.

BIRD
By yourself? As young as you are?

RAVE
When you think about it, we've always gone over by ourselves. My mind went once; my heart went another time; now all parts of me are going this time.

BIRD
And so now you're not afraid? All this talk about going over there was for nothing?

RAVE
No way, Bird. There's always that fear. The fear I'll never come back as one of my people. I wasn't joking when I said I was afraid of coming back white.

BIRD
Your skin would change color? That happens. Tanning happens to some. In the winter your skin can go a little paler. But just because you are part white doesn't mean your skin will go completely white once you acknowledge it. My skin hasn't gone completely black.

RAVE
No. Not my skin, but my mind and heart, what's inside of me would change.

BIRD
It would change color?

RAVE
No. It . . . it would be different, hard to describe, confusing in a way. I don't have the words.

BIRD
Sounds like it's already started.

RAVE
There are always words for these things, but I, I . . .

BIRD
You never learned them. Or maybe we don't have these words in our tongue. We don't always have the same things as they do over there, and that includes words. It will be interesting to see if you will you learn them over there? You aren't doing so hot here.

RAVE
I guess I'm just as bad as some of my cousins. I remember we had this one white-looking cousin who was speaking to us in our language, and he wasn't even from us. He was from a different group. He was so happy he stumped us. Someone taught him how to speak.

BIRD
Did you young guys get mad? Tune him up for it?

RAVE
Nah, we just listened to what he said. It sounded good, but his actions later proved his words meant nothing. I'm afraid that could be me one of these days while I'm over there.

BIRD
What made his words so weak?

RAVE
He talked about respect, but when Gloria and her friends came over, he talked to them in a really bad way. After he called them "sisters," too.

BIRD
Sounds like he was a lower-class warrior guy.

[*A light flashes from across the river bank.*]

RAVE
What is that?

BIRD
You'll have to go soon.

RAVE
Are they calling me?

BIRD
Yes, but listen to me, Rave. You know what you are. You know we are a part of you; you have us with you always, and you know what we are to you. This is more than what some of them over there have. No matter what is said to you, no matter who questions you, don't ever let that go. No matter how hard they try to tear that from you. Hang on tight to it. They will try to take a lot from you but hold on. No matter how dark it gets over there. When you look and question why we are even here, why you are even a part of us, remember that if you keep holding on to that belief that you are one of us, it will grow, and it will hold on to you. No matter where you cross, where you go, we will always be there because you are a part of us. You might not have any fancy dress, or have any decorative thing to wear, maybe all you will have is just a breath, but it will be enough. You remember this, Rave.

RAVE
So, I guess, I'll have to fight too, huh? Is that how you got all those scars and nicks?

BIRD
Those are just the ones you can see—aye!

RAVE
Aw, I thought you were being serious, Bird.

BIRD
You know you can't be over here. You have to laugh once in a while.

RAVE
What about over there? Can we laugh over there too?

BIRD
You'd better. You won't come back if you don't.

[*Another light flashes.*]

RAVE
Well, I guess I'll go then. I'll go and see what it's like over there.

BIRD
You have everything?

RAVE
I even have my enrollment card.

BIRD
You know you won't need that, but that's always good to have to intimidate the weak of being. Especially when you run into those who have nothing else and they try to bully you.

RAVE
I won't do that. It's just—I don't have a real ID.

BIRD
Then you better apply for one.

RAVE
You'll follow me, Bird?

BIRD
As long as I can, and when I can. I'll be there for you.

RAVE
Then let's move.

BIRD
Your parents were right, Rave. You are the bold one of your family. Or was it the goofy one?

RAVE
I'm the one who wasn't doing anything over here. I'll see if I can get into anything over there.

BIRD
Nothing? Not evening snagging, or snagged?

RAVE
Nope. I have nothing to leave on this side, but a lot of myself. I have a lot of myself over there I have to find.

BIRD
Just don't forget to share, *aye!*

RAVE
I bet they don't say that over there, or enit. Enit?

[*They begin to cross over.*]

BIRD
No frybread, but they do know about Spam and fried baloney.

RAVE
The classics, *aye!* Maybe this will be good for me. It's a new path. I'm not sure where we are supposed to . . .

[BIRD *exits.*]

Bird? Bird? Shoot! By myself again.

Blackout. End of play.

It Came from Across the Big Pond

Production Note: This is based on the 1950s sci-fi "invasion" films genre. It is important to find the moments that can be played big, as well as subtle melodramatic moments.

Characters

MYRON JACKSON
BETSY TWO ROBES
ERNIE JACKSON
AUNTIE CAROL
PROCESSORS #1, #2, and #3
JEFF

Setting

Time: Could be present day
Place: A home on a western reservation in Montana

The home of the Jackson family. It is a modest two-bedroom house that serves a family of eight. MYRON JACKSON *is asleep on the couch. There is a huge flash of light and an explosion. He wakes up.*

MYRON
What the—?

[*Looks around the room.*]

Ma? Ernie? Betsy?

[*He gets up from the couch.*]

Where is every—?

[ERNIE *and* BETSY *enter the room in a hurry slamming the door behind them.*]

What're you guys doing?

ERNIE
Myron! Gee. Myron!

MYRON
What's wrong with you?

BETSY
Something's happening, Myron!

ERNIE
Wait, let's be sure it's him first.

[ERNIE *crosses to* MYRON.]

Are you Myron Jackson?

MYRON
What?

ERNIE
Are you Myron Jackson?

MYRON
Yeah.

ERNIE
Cousin to Peter Nygaurd, or first cousin?

MYRON
What?

ERNIE
Cousin, or first cousin to Peter?

MYRON
Yeah, I claim him as my cousin.

BETSY
Oh good. It's Myron.

ERNIE
Wait, you can't be sure.

[*He slaps* MYRON.]

MYRON
You little sh—!

[ERNIE *runs behind* BETSY *for cover.*]

ERNIE
Okay? Okay? Okay? Yeah, it's him!

BETSY
Myron, Myron, stop. We had to be sure it's you.

MYRON
What the hell is going on?

ERNIE
We don't know.

MYRON
And you slapped me for what reason?

BETSY
No. Listen, Myron. Something is very wrong.

MYRON
First off, I let this little turd hit me.

BETSY
No. People are changing.

MYRON
Changing. You mean clothes?

ERNIE
No. There are these guys walking around dressed in dress pants and shirts—

MYRON
Mormon missionaries, they always walk around—

ERNIE
No. They have black suits on—

MYRON
Jehovah's Witnesses—

ERNIE
Will you listen! They aren't missionaries, or Witnesses, or FBI.

MYRON
Well, what are they then?

BETSY
We don't know.

MYRON
What? Are you guys smoking something?

BETSY
No.

ERNIE
No, not recently. Okay, okay. No!

MYRON
So you have some guys in suits walking around the projects. That isn't anything new.

BETSY
Yes, but when they go into a house the family disappears, and when they show up they are completely different.

MYRON
Don't lie!

ERNIE
It's not funny. Stop laughing, Myron. She's telling you the truth.

MYRON
How are people changing?

BETSY
Vic Chambers. They went into his house, and after an hour he came out with all his dance outfit stuff, his camping things, his teepee poles—

ERNIE
Put all his things on a pile and set it on fire. He even stood there and cut his braids.

MYRON
Don't lie.

ERNIE
I'm not. I saw it. When I asked him what he was doing, he just stood there and looked at me and asked me if—this is weird—but he asked me if I would like to join him for some refreshing Kool-Aid and tuna fish sandwiches.

MYRON
His dancing outfit? All of it? The eagle feather bustle too?

ERNIE
All of it. Then he started to talk about how he had to trim his lawn and maybe he should buy some of those little plastic gnomes at the hardware store. He took a weed chopper to those big sage bushes out in his backyard. And, and, Starvin' Marvin . . .

MYRON
They went to see him?

ERNIE
Yes. He picked up his fancy backrest, his makeshift sweat, and loaded it all into his trailer and drove off.

MYRON
Well, he wasn't from our people, so that isn't really anything new. Maybe he found people who would adopt him.

ERNIE
And the smoke shack?

MYRON
What about it?

BETSY
They were in there last night. And this morning, they turned it into a milk bar.

MYRON
Milk bar? They sell chocolate milk? I could go for some chocolate milk right about now.

BETSY
I went in there this morning and there are two of them behind the counter, wearing suits and sunglasses. They sell only milk. White milk. Whole milk, 2 percent, 1 percent, skim milk, but it is all white. No chocolate, no strawberry milk.

ERNIE
Damn. Scary, huh?

MYRON
Did they buy it? You didn't see Buck Flynn . . .

BETSY
He drove up in a red Toyota. He wasn't driving his big rig Ford. He was wearing slacks, slippers, and a sweater.

MYRON
Buck?

[*There is a knock at the door. They freeze.*]

ERNIE
Don't, don't, don't answer it.

MYRON
Why?

BETSY
It could be them.

[*More knocking.*]

ERNIE
Myron, no.

[AUNTIE CAROL's *voice from the kitchen.*]

AUNTIE CAROL

[*Offstage.*]

Myron, get the door.

MYRON
What should I do? I'll go see.

[*He goes to a window.*]

BETSY
Is it them?

MYRON
I don't know. They look like well-dressed Mormons.

[*Knocking on the door again.*]

AUNTIE CAROL

[*Offstage.*]

Get the door!

ERNIE
I'll go. Keep Auntie Carol quiet.

[*He exits.*]

BETSY
Don't open it, Myron.

MYRON
Wait, wait, let me see.

[*He opens the door.*]

VOICE OF VISITOR

[*Offstage.*]

Hello. Can I talk to you today about being assimilated into the kingdom of . . .

MYRON
Not today!

[MYRON *slams the door.*]

BETSY
Myron, that was pretty cool.

[*Voices of* ERNIE *and* AUNTIE CAROL *offstage.*]

ERNIE

[*Offstage.*]

Auntie Carol, you are the cousin to my mom, or third cousin?

AUNTIE CAROL

[*Offstage.*]

We don't count our . . .

[*Sounds of two loud slaps and* ERNIE *runs in followed by* AUNTIE CAROL.]

ERNIE
Okay? Okay? Okay? Yeah. All right.

BETSY
What's wrong, Auntie Carol?

AUNTIE CAROL
This little turd tried to slap me in the kitchen. I stopped him and slapped him. I think I'm going give him a couple of good hard ones to remember.

ERNIE
Sorry, sorry, but look at her? I thought they got to her, and she's changing.

AUNTIE CAROL
I'm cooking frybread! Now I need to go back there before I burn anything. Myron. Keep this one in here.

MYRON
Yes, Auntie. You're lucky my uncle isn't here.

ERNIE
I thought she was changing. I didn't even think of the frybread.

BETSY
You didn't smell the grease? Smell the flour?

ERNIE
I wasn't thinking about it, okay?

MYRON
She decked you, huh?

ERNIE
No. Yeah.

BETSY
Do you think those guys will come back?

MYRON
I don't know. They didn't look that strange. Are you two sure there is something going on, and these guys are the reason for it?

BETSY
Yeah. It's like everybody is losing a part of themselves.

ERNIE
They change, Myron. They just aren't the same.

MYRON
In this short of time?

BETSY
It's happening all over, Myron. My cousin in Wolf Point said everybody got rid of their dance outfits and burned them. They torn down things that were Indin.

ERNIE
I heard some people who had those huge satellite dishes in front of their houses went out and pointed those dishes straight up into the sky.

MYRON
And dogs are starting to talk.

ERNIE
Really? Where'd you hear that?

MYRON
I haven't. I'm just making it up.

ERNIE
Oh. Well don't do that. There are a lot of strange things happening, Myron.

[AUNTIE CAROL *enters with two large paper bags with newly formed grease spots. She wears a scarf and has her purse.*]

AUNTIE CAROL
I'm taking these over to the community hall. When I get back, I'll clean the kitchen. Myron, I want you to clean up out back. Get your motorbike parts straightened out. I don't want any of these kids hurting themselves.

MYRON
All right.

BETSY
Auntie Carol.

AUNTIE CAROL
What Betsy?

BETSY
You can't go!

AUNTIE CAROL
What's wrong with you, Betsy?

BETSY
Uh, the community hall is closed.

AUNTIE CAROL
I know. I'm going to open it when I get there.

ERNIE
Wait . . .

AUNTIE CAROL
You stay here.

ERNIE
We heard there's a busted water pipe and they're trying to fix it. Right now.

AUNTIE CAROL
No one told me. Did anybody call, Myron?

MYRON
No. I'll check the phone.

[*Crosses to a wall and picks up the receiver of the phone.*]

No signal.

ERNIE
The lines are down. See. They are doing all kinds of work.

AUNTIE CAROL
Well, I should go over and see.

BETSY
We can. Just stay here, Auntie Carol. We'll run over there in an hour and see what's happening.

ERNIE
Yeah.

AUNTIE CAROL
Well, I'll go and try to keep this bread warm.

ERNIE
I'll help. No? Okay, okay . . .

AUNTIE CAROL
You stay in here. Let me know when you kids are going to go. I think I might read.

   [*She exits.*]

MYRON
Why'd you say that?

BETSY
Keep her here, just in case.

MYRON
In case of what?

ERNIE
Those guys.

MYRON
This is getting messed up. I don't know if I should . . .

   [*Someone knocks on the door.*]

BETSY
It's them!

ERNIE
Hide!

MYRON
Hide? If it's them, they know we are here.

ERNIE
Oh yeah, huh?

BETSY
Are you going to open it, Myron?

ERNIE
You have any weapons?

MYRON
Weapons? Like what?

ERNIE
You got to have something.

[*Digs into a nearby cardboard box.*]

Like, like, an old envelope, some duck tape, electrician's tape, an old deer bone . . .

MYRON
Ernie! Knock it off!

[*Knock on the door again.*]

BETSY
Wait, wait . . .

[*Runs into the kitchen area and picks up a small iron skillet.*]

I'm ready.

MYRON
What're you going to do with that? Make them some fried baloney?

ERNIE
I want some . . .

BETSY
Just open the door.

MYRON
Count of three. Three, two . . .

JEFF
One.

[JEFF, *a deputy assimilation processor, enters with three other* PROCESSORS.]

ERNIE
Get 'em!

[ERNIE *charges and stops because he is the only one charging.*]

MYRON
Sit down.

JEFF
Hello . . . Myron Blue, yes?

[*He holds a small notebook.*]

MYRON
Yeah.

JEFF
And you are Betsy Two Robes? Ernie Jackson?

MYRON
Who are you?

JEFF
You, you, go check the back, you can start looking in that area. Remove anything that may impede the process.

MYRON
Hey! What's going on?

JEFF
You have the last house in the neighborhood. You've been selected for social gentrification and assimilation.

MYRON
What?

BETSY
They want to turn us white.

ERNIE
No! Oh god, no! I can't turn white! My relatives.

MYRON
You're part white now, Ernie.

ERNIE
Oh yeah, huh?

MYRON
So am I.

BETSY
I'm not.

JEFF
Yes, unfortunately our program doesn't include you. You'll have to come with us.

MYRON
Why?

JEFF
This process will be simple and easier for you and him, but since she isn't, how does one say this, similar to you. We'll have to take her to the center for a more intense process.

ERNIE
I didn't know Betsy was a full blood.

BETSY
I'm part black.

JEFF
Difficult to assimilate, both races are difficult. If you were more like other ethnics, the process wouldn't be so difficult.

PROCESSOR #2
We've found seventy-five percent of the personal materials will have to be removed.

MYRON
Removed? Wait. You guys are going to take our stuff?

JEFF
Let's remove them first before you start resource removal.

MYRON
We aren't going anywhere!

[BETSY *crosses to* MYRON.]

BETSY
Help me, Myron? Don't let them take me.

MYRON
Ernie, get over here. You aren't removing anyone from this house.

JEFF
Myron, you two others, don't be so confrontational. This has happened so many times before throughout history. In fact, I know your Auntie Carol has gone through it once in her life.

MYRON
What are you talking about?

JEFF
Assimilation. Myron, this process is very subtle today. It isn't like in the past where people were starved, re-educated, infected, kidnapped, or murdered. This is a very gentle process where your people give up a little more of yourself and those around you, so you can join the larger community. You want that, don't you? It would be so beneficial for you, your family, relatives, and even your friends to move around without any lingering suspicion or doubt.

ERNIE
You mean like going into a store and not be followed?

JEFF
Yes, yes, that is just a minute example of what this will do for you.

ERNIE
We get converted to be white?

JEFF
In a way, but you won't have all that difficult business of being sovereign. Something you people wanted long ago, and when a little of it was given to you there were so many problems created by it. Treaties, agreements—it was huge legal mess. Now we have something new that will help you become better situated in our society.

BETSY
Whose society?

JEFF
Our society. Mine and eventually, your society, too.

MYRON
You don't want us to be Native, or Indin, anymore.

ERNIE
They can't do that? Can they?

JEFF
We wanted you to be a part of us a long time ago. Your people were baptized, inducted, educated, cleaned up, but it didn't do a lot for your development of assimilation. These two new processes will help you regenerate a new interest and move the process along. It isn't going to be painful, a little difficult for her, but we've designed this, again, specifically for your people.

BETSY
Don't let them take me, Myron.

MYRON
I won't.

JEFF
Here.

[PROCESSOR #3 *approaches and hands* JEFF *some photos.*]

This is the new image we have of you. Take a look. I think you'll enjoy them. They tested quite well with forty percent of Americans.

MYRON
What are these?

ERNIE
Are these supposed to be us?

BETSY
They look like everybody else.

JEFF
The way you people should have been over a century ago. Be thankful that we replaced the older processors. Upgrades are good for everybody.

BETSY
I can't look like this.

JEFF
Yes. That's why you have to come with us.

ERNIE
No way! They can't make anyone look this way.

JEFF
We can. Call your aunt.

MYRON
Auntie Carol?

JEFF
Call her. I will. Carol Blue, please enter.

> [AUNTIE CAROL *enters and she looks like a Mary Kay image, dressed in pink; her hair is up and tight.*]

MYRON
What the . . . ?

BETSY
What did you do to her?

ERNIE
She looks like she works at the jewelry section at Penney's.

MYRON
Auntie Carol?

JEFF
She can't talk right now. Her speech component has to be changed and enhanced to provide acceptable female responses.

MYRON
You can't do this! She's a member of the Nakota tribe!

[*All the* PROCESSORS *react to the word.*]

JEFF
Stop that!

BETSY
She is Nakota!

[*The* PROCESSORS *react.*]

JEFF
Stop that. Stop saying that word!

BETSY
Nakota, Lakota, Dakota!

PROCESSORS
Stop! Nonfully assimilated words!

ERNIE
She is Wodopna!

BETSY
We can't be you . . . Oyate!

MYRON
Leave us . . . Oyate!

ERNIE
Yeah. Enit.

MYRON
Enit isn't a traditional word?

ERNIE
Enit? It isn't? Oh! Frybread!

BETSY
That isn't a traditional word or food—*tanigha.*

[MYRON *breaks out into a song. As he sings* ERNIE *and* BETSY *join him. The* PROCESSORS *react, and at the end of* MYRON'*s song the* PROCESSORS *are finished.*]

ERNIE
What did you do?

MYRON
As long as we keep a part of who and what we are—no one will ever change us.

Blackout. End of play.

The Curse of the Tiger Lily Two-Step

Characters

GEORGE WIND
DARLENE SHORTER
EARL SHARPES
OSCAR RIGHTBINKY
DRAMA TEAM
TIGER LILY

Onstage are three movie screens—stage right, stage left, and center stage. A podium is slightly downstage. GEORGE WIND *walks to the podium with a tablet and some file folders filled with papers. He has a revolver.*

GEORGE
Hello. I'm George Wind. I am an investigative journalist for the *Native Newz Circle*. I want to begin this presentation right away because we have some shocking and surprising elements to reveal to you concerning the phenomenon known as the "Tiger Lily Two-Step Curse." This supposed Indin, I mean, "Indian" curse has been repeating itself in the last four years across the country. Please take a seat for those of you who are arriving late. When we dim the lights we will have to secure the doors. Trust me, no one here in this auditorium will be in danger, or any threat of danger, but just to secure the elements we will be revealing today. You will notice we have student volunteers located at every other row with either a flashlight, or a

flashgun. I assure you the flashguns are not for you, or to be used in any way against you. These students are volunteers from the local campus ROTC and the Student Supporters of the Second Amendment—they of course had their own rifles but we want them to use these nonlethal flashlight rifles. Unlike Oprah, all of will not receive your own flashgun.

[*Lights dim.*]

1987, in the late spring, a small non-Tribal affiliate powwow is being held outside of the town of Galvan, Montana. Again, the gathering, or powwow, is not affiliated with any Native Tribe of Montana. In fact, it is referred to as the "Spring Hop Powwow and Rendezvous."

[*First image on screen. People dressed as fur traders and Indians.*]

This event, the "Spring Hop Powwow and Rendezvous," has been an annual event for nearly five years. The final event of this gathering is the reenactment of the town's founder, Landis McSquit, who is attacked and violated by a yearling grizzly bear.

[*Image is acted out by a group of people having their shadows seen on the screen.*]

A reminder for the community members as to the strife and pain they endured to celebrate the theft of stolen land.

[*Image of Landis with bear's arm over his shoulder.*]

It is during an inter-Tribal at the powwow when the first recorded event of the phenomena happened. There was an estimate of over fifty dancers in the dance arena when the event happened. We have a recorded testimony of Earl Sharpes, a local man, who was dancing men's traditional that day. He is being interviewed by investigative member, Darlene Shorter.

[EARL SHARPES *appears in front of the screen. He wears a disheveled dance outfit. He begins to speak in a rugged rustic frontier's voice.*]

EARL
Well, dang nabit! We wuz only doin' it fur . . .

[DARLENE SHORTER *appears, holding a microphone.*]

DARLENE
Pardon me. We don't understand you.

[*She smacks* EARL *on the shoulder.*]

EARL
Ahem, Thank you, Miss. Well, in recalling the day's events, my wife and I thought it would be added fun to our rural lives if we attended the powwow.

DARLENE
This was the first ever "Indian" powwow both of you have attended, yes?

EARL
Yes. We're white, White Americans, and we thought we would do something ethnic. So the missus suggests we should go to the powwow. We made our own dancing costumes and thought it would be a pleasant change for the day. Pretty authentic-looking right?

DARLENE
No. And you had already heard of a possible curse, or warning of some type?

EARL
Yes, miss, we heard a story that this powwow had been cursed. We didn't get the full story of how or what kind of curse had been placed on the powwow, but as I said before, we're white, so if it was an Indian voodoo curse it doesn't bother us, so we went.

DARLENE
So you went to this powwow. I'm curious, Mr. Sharpes. Were you and your wife invited to this powwow?

EARL
Invited? You mean like an invitation?

DARLENE
No, like a friend or relative inviting you to attend?

EARL
No. My wife used to be a member of the "Galvan Blood Braves" cheerleading squad when she was in high school, and when she was online she saw this flyer for the powwow. Since she used to cheer for the "Bloody Braves," we thought it would be kind of interesting to attend.

DARLENE
So, based on a connection to a stereotype mascot you both decided to venture here?

EARL
Well, don't get too much of an attitude about it, but yeah.

DARLENE
Sorry, not my attitude, just a nonwhite reality. So what happened next?

EARL
It was when we heard the call of an inter-Tribal dance. I thought, "Damn, I don't want to be out here dancing with a bunch of refugees."

DARLENE
And were they?

EARL
No. I saw it was nothing but a bunch of our folks, so I went out to dance. That's all I can remember.

[*Lights up on* GEORGE.]

GEORGE
No one knew what happened during that inter-Tribal dance. Some blamed refugees, but since there were no refugees there what happened next is unexplained. We were able to find a recording of the event taken by the local high school booster club's video camera. Here is what was captured on film.

[*On center-stage screen an image of dancers appears. Film begins and it is out of focus. When the film focuses we see a group of non-Native dancers. It is a Boy Scout Indian jamboree film. All of a sudden the dancers speed up to a point of being uncontrollable and the film breaks and dissolves.*]

DARLENE
What you don't see in this film is, according to eyewitnesses, a small person appears in the film, out of frame, in the center of the arena.

GEORGE
The figure is supposedly a female. Standing about two and half to three feet tall.

DARLENE
Eyewitnesses say the figure is dressed as a Native American, but no specific Tribe. A few Native Tribal people were in attendance at the powwow, but some were just vending and some were just trying to snag.

GEORGE
Really? Oh. But they couldn't offer any Tribal identification of the figure. Some witnesses say the figure was dressed like an Indian. Other say the figure's skin was nearly a pure ivory. Others say, if it was in winter, they would have never seen it. Still others comment about the figure's coal-black hair. There is a story of an elderly woman who attempted to reach out to touch the figure's hair, but overextended her reach and fell, being trampled by so many Minnetonka moccasins.

DARLENE
Is this a case of paranormal activity? A case of mass hysteria regarding personal and social fears focused into a creation of a mysterious figure to be feared? Gee, and it has to be an Indin, again.

GEORGE
The "Tiger Lily Two-Step Curse" is born. It carries on for several years. Traveling across Western United States without stopping, but with a strong appearance during spring and summer powwow, fairs, and rendezvouses.

DARLENE
They say it's a curse, but no Tribe is blamed for it.

GEORGE
Nor are any Tribes coming forward to take responsibility for it.

DARLENE
I interviewed an elderly Native man from Missoula, Montana about the curse. Here is a part of that interview.

[*On the screen is an elderly Native man,* OSCAR, *right.*]

DARLENE [*Voice over.*]
How did you first hear of the "Tiger Lily Two-Step Curse"?

OSCAR
I used to run a burger stand at the summer powwow for my girl. One night, after everybody was closing down, this young white guy, oh, what do they call them now, Rainbow, yeah, Rainbow Child came to my stand.

DARLENE
Rainbow Child? What was he doing there?

OSCAR
He wanted to trade me a hank of beads for a hamburger.

DARLENE
And did you?

OSCAR
No. He might have stole them. You know how they are. They weren't even store bought. He must've gathered all together and strung them himself. He was really hungry. I'm glad no one else was around.

DARLENE
Because he was white?

OSCAR
No. Because he stinks? Remember? Those Rainbow Children don't bathe that often. He made that old hamburger grease smell good.

DARLENE
And you told him the story of the "Tiger Lily Two-Step Curse"?

OSCAR
No. He told me. He said they were having a big dance one night, and out of the woods came this little Indian person. At first I thought it was a "Little Person"—oh. I shouldn't talk about that.

DARLENE
That's all right, but tell us what he told you.

OSCAR
Well, I don't think he would know what a "Little Person" is, but he said this little Indian thingy came out of the woods. All of a sudden he said there were these songs that played really loud. Scared everybody.

DARLENE
Songs? Drum or flute?

OSCAR
He didn't really say, but he said, "The trees opened up, all these magic creatures came out and danced with them until the sunrise."

DARLENE
Did you believe him?

OSCAR
No, but they take a lot of drugs, so it could be true in their reality. White people are always seeing things they don't know what they are looking at and go nuts.

DARLENE
Do you think this is a curse?

OSCAR
A curse? What?

DARLENE
Some people are saying this is an old Indian curse against those who make fun or steal from Indin people.

OSCAR
I'd keep it up just to make them behave, but this isn't a curse.

DARLENE
How do you know?

OSCAR
Our way is to be thankful and to help others. We wouldn't pray for something bad against another person. That's not right. No matter how bad we've been treated, we always take good from the bad. This is not from the creator, I don't think.

DARLENE
They are blaming it on the Indins.

OSCAR
Indins, Blacks, Mexicans, Asians, all those who aren't white always get the blame when something goes bad. You know this. You weren't always in school.

DARLENE
Yeah, thank you for your time uncle—I mean, Mr. Right.

OSCAR
Yes. You are welcome, my girl—ohh! Shouldn't have said that, huh?

[*Screen goes to white and lights up on* GEORGE.]

GEORGE
And now the highlight of our presentation. Last month, at an authentic dance rally to support the University Rocky Warriors, our investigative team attended to confront this would-be curse. Darlene, myself, and a few other assistants attended with an eclectic reserve of tools.

DARLENE
Our goal at first seemed a little bit cliché. It was like all the other paranormal groups, but we aren't a paranormal group. We weren't just going to film and record some sounds and images.

GEORGE
If this would-be "Indian figure" were to appear. We were going to capture it.

DARLENE
And unfortunately, during the event, all our recording devices were broken.

GEORGE
So, to give you an idea of what happened, we've asked the high school drama team to reenact that once in a life time event.

[*A group of white high school actors appear onstage.*]

DARLENE
We want to thank the Galvan High School Drama team. Binky? Are you and your group ready?

BINKY
"Ensemble."

DARLENE
All right, "Binky."

[*Stage lights up. The drama team takes center stage.*]

GEORGE
Like reports from past events. The dance rally began with what the University considered an "Indian dance" with "real" Indians.

[*Students do an "Indian dance."*]

At the high point, the team's mascot, "Willie the Wily Warrior," was to appear at one of the gyms and head to the center of the gym floor.

DARLENE
Once Willie Warrior reaches the center of the gym, the young "Indian" maidens would then encircle him offering their maiden-ness to the powerful Willy . . . Oh brother.

GEORGE
Hang in there, Darlene! Just when this happened, the lights went out of control flashing off and on.

[*Lights do this.*]

The little "Indian figure" appeared at the foul line. We rushed onto the gym floor with flashlights, ropes, and duck tape.

DARLENE
Here now is the actual audio recording of that event from someone's phone.

VOICES

[*Offstage*]

What the hell is that . . . ?
Is isn't an Indin!
Looks like Luke's cousin!
Grab it!
It bit me!
Wait, flash your light! It's afraid of the light! Use your flashlights and create a box barrier. A box barrier around it, not me.
Oh! Sorry . . .
Here, here, use this box.
The box is pretty weak!
Use the duck tape and tape it!
Go around it!
I wish that music would stop!

[*Tape ends and lights up. Onstage is a large cardboard box wrapped in duck tape. There are wooden poles on the two sides of the box for carrying it.*]

DARLENE
We are now pleased to bring to you the entity of the "Tiger Lily Two-Step Curse" . . . Please, remain seated. Do not scream, or make any loud noises.

GEORGE
Since we are not at a real Native Tribal celebration, I'm sure none of you will take photos or record this event at this point forward.

[*The cardboard box begins to shake and slightly bounce.*]

We will need some assistance here. Let's have our light cage activated.

[*Four bright lights appear on the corners of the box.*]

DARLENE
Please, no flashes.

GEORGE
All right, Darlene. Could you please take your microphone and go to the box.

DARLENE
What?

GEORGE
Go to the box.

DARLENE
Why me?

GEORGE
Well, because, you know.

DARLENE
Know what?

GEORGE
You're a woman.

DARLENE
Yeah. What has that got to do with me going to this thing in the damn box?

GEORGE
It's, um, it's a female.

DARLENE
So?

GEORGE
You might be able to, you know, connect with it.

DARLENE
I'll connect my foot with your—! Get over here, George!

[GEORGE *and* DARLENE *approach the box.*]

GEORGE
Hello? Hi?

[*No answer.* GEORGE *moves closer.*]

Hello.

[DARLENE *kicks the box. The box shakes and a sharp scream is heard.*]

Don't do that!

DARLENE
Don't be afraid. What are you?

TIGER LILY
Tiger Lily.

GEORGE
What?

TIGER LILY
Tiger Lily.

DARLENE
What are you?

TIGER LILY
I'm an Indian.

DARLENE
No, you're not.

TIGER LILY
I'm perfect.

DARLENE
Tiger Lily? From *Peter Pan* Tiger Lily?

TIGER LILY
Yes. Is Peter there?

GEORGE
No.

DARLENE
What?

GEORGE
No!

[*The box shakes.*]

DARLENE
Calm down. There is no Peter Pan here.

GEORGE
What are you?

DARLENE
She said she was an Indian, remember? What Tribe, or Nation are you from?

TIGER LILY
Forever Land, I'm a member of the Magic Kingdom.

GEORGE
"Magic Kingdom"? Disney. Do you mean Disney?

DARLENE
You're not real.

TIGER LILY
They made me an Indian. They said I was to be the perfect Indian princess.

DARLENE
Indian princess? For who?

TIGER LILY
People.

DARLENE
People? People of America?

TIGER LILY
All people, Indians, Coloreds . . .

DARLENE
Oh, hell no . . . People of America?

TIGER LILY
They told me I am the perfect Indian.

GEORGE
Is that why you've come to these events? To show off how perfect you are?

TIGER LILY
To celebrate the look of Indian people.

GEORGE
Do you know the people doing the "look of Indian people" are not Indian?

TIGER LILY
They are me.

DARLENE
You are not Indian.

TIGER LILY
Yes, I am. I'm a perfect Indian. I was made to represent all Indian people. When people talk about Indian people, they will think of me and all my beauty. Let me show you.

GEORGE
Are you ready?

DARLENE
Yeah.

[GEORGE *opens the box.* TIGER LILY *appears. (A puppet can be used.)*]

TIGER LILY
Look at me. I'm the perfect Indian.

DARLENE
But you weren't created by Indians.

TIGER LILY
What do you mean?

GEORGE
You're like the name "Indian." "Indian," the word, doesn't come from any of the Native Tribal Indigenous people. It comes from white people.

DARLENE
Like you. You are white—man-made.

TIGER LILY
No. No, I'm a real Indian!

[*She moves around trying to escape.*]

GEORGE
The lights are holding her. Look. You can't escape. You have to face the truth.

TIGER LILY
Release me! Release me now!

DARLENE
Flashlights ready! Everyone!

TIGER LILY
Release me, or I'll call the others!

GEORGE
What others?

DARLENE
Who knows? But get ready, George!

TIGER LILY
Help . . .

[*Her "help" is the same word from the cartoon, but loud and repeating. As she does this at other parts of the stage, the screens split open and every Indian mascot appears. Chief Wahoo, Blackhawks, Chiefs, Redskins, Braves, and other mascots and logos come dancing out and form a circle. Music is heard. First is the song "Why Does the Red Man Say Ugh," commercial drumbeats, and then a few songs and lyrics from* Pocahontas. DARLENE *shines her flashlight on one of the mascots and it falls down.*]

GEORGE
What do we do?

DARLENE
Use your light! Shine your light on them.

GEORGE
Everybody. Hit them with your light!

DARLENE
Don't let any of them escape!

GEORGE
Folks, don't let them get into your mind!

DARLENE
Close your eyes if you have to!

[*The carnage grows as mascots fall. The music slowly dies down and* TIGER LILY *is onstage in a circle of fallen mascots.*]

GEORGE
Hold up! Hold on! Don't shine your light on her!

DARLENE
Everybody! Stop!

TIGER LILY
No . . .

DARLENE
You have to go.

TIGER LILY
I want to stay . . . I want to stay Indian . . .

DARLENE
Not here. Not for us. You can't be here because you are not a part of us. You can't represent us. You were created to represent a lie, a fantasy.

TIGER LILY
I don't hurt anyone . . . I'm good . . .

DARLENE
You are a lie, but not even a good lie. You hurt because you blind the minds of people. You place lies in the hearts of people.

TIGER LILY
I, I, I have to go?

DARLENE
Yes.

TIGER LILY
Let me dance for you?

DARLENE
No. No more dancing like an Indian.

TIGER LILY
No. This is my own dance. I've always wanted to dance this way for a long time but they wouldn't let me.

GEORGE
Let her, Darlene.

DARLENE
All right.

> [TIGER LILY, *the puppet, dances a special dance that is not fake, but has meaning to it. When she is done, she slowly crumples to the floor, lifeless.*]

GEORGE
Gee, if they were all this easy.

DARLENE
If they were, we would all be human.

Blackout. End of play.

One Step In

Characters

FRED, a full-blood Indian
ROGER, an attendant
KELLY, an attendant

ROGER *stands near a large wooden box tossing pieces of clothing, jewelry, and shoes out of the box.* FRED *approaches* ROGER *hobbling on a crutch. They are both dressed in white robes.*

FRED
Uh, hello.

ROGER
Hello. How can I help you?

FRED
I've arrived. I'm here.

ROGER
Oh? Oh! Oh . . . right, here. No. You aren't at the place you think you are.

FRED
Isn't this, you know, "pearly gates" and all.

ROGER
They "used" to be pearly, but we had to pawn the pearls to repair all the damage done down below over the past hundred years. We're using Saran Wrap, but it does shine when the sun hits it.

FRED
Well, I'm here.

ROGER
Right . . . This is a preway station. Oh! Not to worry. It isn't like this is a Mormon setup. God, we'd all be out of jobs if that belief were true. Be thankful for cults.

FRED
Why am I not going through? Why do I have to wait?

[*A second worker enters carrying a stuffed horse. The worker approaches* ROGER.]

ROGER
Hold on. What?

[*Second worker whispers to* ROGER.]

No, Kelly, he wants a real horse, not his toy horse.

KELLY
Do you know how heavy a horse is? Damn humans.

ROGER
Don't worry. Kelly has it handled. Now, your initial check. Name?

FRED
Frederick Runs About.

ROGER
Day of death?

FRED
I, uh, I think it was on February 23? I think? I'm not sure.

ROGER
Wait, you do know you are dead, don't you? You have to be sure. No wandering about up here. You go where we send you.

FRED
No. I'm pretty sure I passed . . . passed away.

ROGER
It takes a while, but it gets easier as we go along. Now, religion?

FRED
I used to be Catholic.

ROGER
Right. Catholic, and then you started going back to your traditional Native Tribal spirituality, didn't you?

FRED
What's wrong? Is that bad?

ROGER
For the Catholics. Miss bingo nights.

FRED
Whoa, is that the one true church?

ROGER
No. There is no "true church," those are all man-made. Glancing over your paperwork we have everything in order.

    [KELLY *enters pulling a tram full of suitcases. He goes to the edge of the stage and slowly starts tossing suitcases over the edge of the stage.*]

FRED
What's, what's Kelly doing?

ROGER
Excess baggage. Kelly's returning it down below.

FRED
Hell?

KELLY
Trump Tower.

ROGER
Well, we have nearly completed your initial interview. Anything I should add, or include?

FRED
Well. I'm a full-blood Native American Indian.

ROGER
No. You can't claim that?

FRED
Why? My mother and father were full bloods.

ROGER
Yes. You used that information as a weapon against those who weren't full-blooded. Instead of celebrating that, you used it as a weapon.

FRED
Does this mean I can't come in? Why not? What's changed?

ROGER
You are using one of our crutches here because down below in your previous life you lost your foot ten years ago.

FRED
Well, yeah, God took it with diabetes.

ROGER
God didn't take it. Isn't that right, Kelly?

KELLY
Yeah, God didn't take it. Has over several billions of pairs.

FRED
Because I'm disabled I can't enter?

ROGER
No. You lost your foot, so you can't claim to be full blood.

FRED
What!

ROGER
Ironic, isn't it? After all those years of harassing those who didn't share the same blood quantum as you, you can't claim what you used against others. According to your records, that's why you divorced your first wife. Belinda. She was part African American and you didn't want to be with her, or the two kids you created.

KELLY
Jerk.

[*They look at* KELLY. KELLY *pauses then points below.*]

FRED
Well, wait, find my foot. A minister told me God took my foot.

ROGER
Kelly? Have you seen this man's foot?

[KELLY *crosses to the box and looks inside.*]

KELLY
Nah. No foot.

ROGER
You had gangrene. God doesn't take feet. Your surgeon removed the foot. And the surgical team who performed the surgery isn't due here for another twenty years, and I doubt they are still carrying it with them.

FRED
If I can't claim to be a full blood? How do I enter?

ROGER
Well.

KELLY
We can give you another foot?

FRED
Someone else's foot?

ROGER
It won't make you a "full blood" according to man-made standards, but you can enter.

KELLY
Hold on.

[KELLY *exits and wheels another wooden box onstage.*]

Here now, we have this one.

[*Holds up a buffalo hoof.*]

This one is a nice little number, snazzy and quiet when you walk.

[*Holds up a cougar's paw.*]

And this one is waterproof.

[*Holds up a duck's webbed foot.*]

FRED
But these aren't human.

ROGER
Right, but they are the only ones we have available.

FRED
Will these make me full-blooded?

ROGER
No, but they will make it easier for you to get around here. No more stumbling or hobbling about with a crutch for you.

FRED
Are you making fun of me?

ROGER/KELLY
No, yes. Maybe.

ROGER
But you want to get in, don't you? Not waiting at a low-level initial waiting area like the Mormons.

FRED
When I get to where I need to go, this foot will change?

ROGER/KELLY
Yeah, maybe.

FRED
I can enter if I wear one of these?

ROGER
Take you to paradise, right along with your relatives.

FRED
What if they see me? With this thing?

ROGER
They'll be happy to see you. To know that you made it.

KELLY
Bingo at nights. No pull tabs though.

FRED
All right. I'll take that one.

KELLY
Good. Waterproof and great for swimming across that river.

[FRED *struggles place the webfoot on his leg.*]

FRED
I can enter now?

ROGER
Yes.

[FRED *walks off slapping the floor with his new foot.*]

KELLY
You think we'll get into trouble for this one?

ROGER
No. He learned a lesson, so she won't be mad. Just let her see him. She needs a laugh.

Blackout. End of play.

Notes

1. Albert Schweitzer, "The Goethe of India," March 16, 2018, http://www.havardsquarelibrary/biographies/rabindranath-tagore-poet-of-power-the-goethe-of-india/; Saul Bellow, "Papuans and Zulus," *New York Times*, March 10, 1994, accessed March 16, 2018, https://arrchive.nytimes.com/www.nytimes.com/books/00/04/23/specials/bellow-papuans.html.

2. Birgit Däwes, "William S. Yellow Robe, Jr.," in *The Methuen Drama Guide to Contemporary American Playwrights*, ed. Martin Middeke, et al. (London: Bloomsbury, 2014), 461.

3. Ibid.

4. Paulette Beete, "Art Talk with William S. Yellow Robe, Jr.," April 8, 2014, accessed March 18, 2018, https://www.arts.gov/art-works/2014/art-talk-william-s-yellow-robe-jr. Yellow Robe told the interviewer, "Ironically, years later when I had my first professional reading with the Native American Theatre Ensemble in L.A. with Hanay Geiogamah—this way back in 1985–1986, in December—I got an envelope in the mail one day and it contained the two plays I wrote for . . . sixth-grade elementary class." Ibid.

5. Yellow Robe, *Where the Pavement Ends*, vii.

6. It was later discovered that an accountant had embezzled $293,000. Richard Chang, "Institute of American Indian Arts Looks to the Future, *Tribal College* 10, no. 1 (fall 1998), tribalcollegejournal.org/institute-american-indian-arts-future/.

7. Yellow Robe, *Where the Pavement Ends*, viii–ix

8. Lukens, *Grandchildren of the Buffalo Soldiers*, xxi.

9. Most Americans believe the Indian Wars were fought by the blindingly white, Anglo-Saxon army of a John Ford Western. In fact, they were fought primarily by German and Irish immigrants and African Americans. The black cavalrymen were known by the Indians as buffalo soldiers. Their infantry counterparts were called "walk-a-heaps."

10. Lukens, *Grandchildren of the Buffalo Soldiers*, xx–xxi.

11. Yellow Robe, *Where the Pavement Ends*, x.

12. Paulette Beete, "Art Talk with William S. Yellow Robe, Jr.," op. cit.

13. Lukens, *Grandchildren of the Buffalo Soldiers*, xii.

www.ingramcontent.com/pod-product-compliance
Lightning Source LLC
Chambersburg PA
CBHW031430160426
43195CB00010BB/680